TORT REFORM

A Study in Frustration

D1622542

TORT
REFORM

A STUDY IN FRUSTRATION

JAMES K. NORMAN

ROCKLIN, CALIFORNIA

Frustration Press, Rocklin, CA, 95667

Editing by Laura Garwood

Book design by Vinnie Kinsella

Cover design by Olivia Croom

ISBN: 978-0-692-11529-9

To Martin A. Harmon,
who inspired the writing of this book

To my beloved wife, La Donna,
who has kept me alive long enough to write it

Table of Contents

Foreword

Martin A. Harmon, a client of over thirty years and a close personal friend, called inquiring whether I knew of someone who would write a book on tort reform. Of course I said I would, and although personal injury was not my specialty in the practice of law, ego sent caution out the window.

About a year later, I find writing is hard, and after retirement, I am not the same person who kept two and a half secretaries busy at the height of my thirty-seven years in the practice of law. Today if I were so foolish as to reenter the ring, I might be able to keep one secretary busy part-time.

Writing a trial brief or an appellate brief, although good training, is far different from writing useful literature someone might choose to read, let alone find interesting. In this effort, I have, for the most part, shunned regurgitating full citations of case authority when dealing with hornbook law; however, I have repeatedly relied upon citations from *A Concise Restatement of Torts*, 3rd edition. The *Restatement* is a good foundation from which we can derive not only what the law today is but what its judicial direction is.

No meaningful discussion of tort reform can be attempted without first bringing the reader up to speed with brief coverage of what a tort is and the history of the judicial environment today. Authorities have generalized the scope of torts as being any wrong from which the law fashions a remedy. This is premised upon our imposing a duty on a person, which is violated, resulting in injury to another. Simply put, liability is based on fault.

I then expand and broaden this imposed duty to encompass warranties by the manufacturer of goods. In setting forth the history of extended liability, I end up with strict liability in tort where liability is imposed on the manufacturer of a hazardous product even though there is no evidence of negligence or intentional wrongdoing.

Chapter 1 is devoted to setting forth a series of problems plaguing the field of torts; in chapter 3, we explore each of the problems. Sandwiched between chapters 1 and 3, chapter 2 is a brief history of today's legal world. Instead of breaking the reader's concentration with lengthy dissertations of cases I have participated in (my war stories), I have attached these cases as appendixes A, B, and C.

There are certain subject areas that warrant separate treatment. I explore the problems we have in the health industry (chapter 4), administrative law (chapter 5), and finally sovereign immunity (chapter 6). The health industry poses unique problems centered around doctors and hospitals and their efforts to provide medical care with ever-increasing government regulations, intervention, and control. Sovereign immunity and administrative law are interrelated, as they deal with government overreaching and lack of accountability for tortious conduct. With sovereign immunity and administrative law, we deal with government improperly roping private property into special districts and imposing taxes on property that cannot benefit from the projects financed by the tax or assessment. This violates the due process protection afforded by the Fifth and Fourteenth Amendments to the Constitution. It also offends the requirement of the payment of just compensation provided for in the Fifth Amendment.

Also in chapter 6, I probe government taking property without offering compensation, let alone just compensation. Finally, I explore *Kelo v. New London* and the issues raised when government—in this case, the City of New London, Connecticut—condemns property on behalf of private interests, in this case, Pfizer Pharmaceutical, for private use, as opposed to for public purpose or use. How does the preceding relate to tort reform? By definition, "any wrong" encompasses tortious conduct on the part of government as well as the private citizen.

In the book's summary, I elaborate on the problems presented and suggest or recommend solutions. My apologies for the occasional slipping into legalese and ponderous detail associated with the case studies. I tried to excise portions, but in doing so, I found the sections lost substantive meaning.

I would like to acknowledge the contributions made to this effort by Martin Harmon, who inspired the writing of the book, and his staff, Allison Murphy; also Laura Garwood, who painstakingly corrected misspellings and grammar in the numerous drafts. Finally, I would not be here but for the efforts of my internist James Drennan and cardiologist Marc Stern, who with my beloved wife, La Donna, have kept me alive for the last two and half decades.

Jim Norman

CHAPTER 1

Introduction to Tort Reform

This is not the first book on tort reform, nor will it be the last. Hopefully it will significantly contribute to addressing the serious problems in that area of the law that deals with the behavioral relationships we have with each other and at times with our government. While it is clear that much good comes from our efforts to dispose of these disputes, in the administration of tort law, we seem to bring out and exhibit the worst of all worlds.

In this book, the reader will find matter highly critical of lawyers, judges, administrative law judges, labor unions, and insurance companies. It is not my intent to cast any of the above groups in a bad light. For the most part, all perform their functions admirably. Unfortunately, some don't. The book reflects my personal experiences during my thirty-seven years of diverse trial practice.

What I try to do in this book is examine the history that has led us to a multitude of problems. I then explore recent dramatic changes in the law concerning torts and related issues. From this point, I introduce select problems, followed by what has already been done to lessen the negative impact of the problems. I make suggestions as to possible further steps to alleviate the impact of the problems and, finally, summarize and draw conclusions from the points made.

I look first at our Article III courts; that is, the court system established in Article III of our Constitution and by state constitutions. These are the local superior courts (the trial courts), the courts of appeal, and the state supreme courts. We have a parallel federal system, consisting of the federal district courts (the trial courts), the circuit courts of appeal, and the United States Supreme Court (hereinafter the USSC). I also discuss what we call the administrative law courts, established under federal and state legislative acts.

The Nature of Torts

The field of torts is man-made law, as opposed to rights and duties created by a contract and enforced by the courts. Torts today are created by legislatures. Being so, most remedies must be through our legislation. However, when a sought-after change will upset the special interests that influenced the legislators who created the law, the chances of significant changes become, at best, difficult. While we may well claim our courts can lead the way, in the final analysis, the Supreme Court justice and the legislator respond to different drummers, with our legislatures ending up with the trump card.

The Scope of Torts

What is the scope of tort law? I start with the premise that we compensate the injured plaintiff, if it be an injury to his person, his property, or his property interests, to make him whole. We visit liability on people who caused the injury. California, in *Denning v. State* (1899) 123 Cal. 323, defines a tort as any wrongful conduct for which the courts can fashion an appropriate remedy. Our courts are here to fashion that appropriate remedy by applying the enacted legislation.

Equitable remedies differ from tort remedies at law. The court may sit at law or in equity. Equity is law that has been generated by courts down through the centuries to, so to speak, fill in the cracks. The equitable remedies of restitution or unjust enrichment are centered on the fundamental premise that one who has been unjustly enriched at the expense of another should make restitution.

This book speaks from the perspective of the consumer, the person hurt, as opposed to the lawyers or judges who administer the law. The American Trial Lawyers and the

American Bar Association, now the American Association for Justice, adequately protect the interests of the lawyers. Unfortunately, the interests of the lawyer and the client diverge and at times are in direct conflict.

The Problems

The overriding principle is that people are supposed to be served by the legal system. The same is true of the other two branches of government. Government's power hinges on the consent of the governed, yet the people to be served justifiably complain. Following are some examples of their concerns:

- It takes too long to get into court, let alone go to trial.
- The process is incredibly expensive.
- My attorney has advised me that even though I am, at best, marginally responsible for the plaintiff's injury, I can be held responsible for the whole of any judgment.
- My attorney and I are aware the plaintiff has been partially compensated, yet my attorney tells me that we cannot disclose this to the jury, facilitating the plaintiff being paid twice for the same injury, the second time at my expense.
- The premium for my liability insurance increased to the point where I must agree to assume liability

for the first $100,000 to decrease the premium to a livable amount. Then, at trial, I find myself at odds with my own attorney (hired by the insurance carrier), who is leaning heavily on me to settle for an amount within that self-insured coverage, thereby relieving the carrier from any exposure.

- Why is it, in case after case, that all sides hire "experts," who, for a fee, with a straight face, testify in accordance with counsel's instructions, each reaching different, at times diametrically opposed, conclusions from the same basic set of facts?

- Why, as a client in multiple-party litigation, do I get the uncomfortable feeling my insurance counsel is too cozy with opposing counsel? Why is it I see on my bill multiple depositions of the same witness at different times? Why is it that each counsel asks the same questions asked previously by other counsel at prior depositions? Why are there the same interrogatories of the same party previously lodged by other sides of the dispute? Why does this practice persist until most of the insurance company's reserve for this dispute is consumed in attorney fees? Until this point is reached, there seems no interest in settling.

- Why is the venue for my case and trial set in Mississippi when I have never been there, conducted business there, or sold any products in Mississippi? I live in California.

- Why is it that the value of this lawsuit has been dramatically changed by the plaintiff simply amending his complaint to throw in a count for punitive damages? What does that additional claim have to do with the lawsuit other than enhancing its value?

- What is going on here? How can I have a fair trial? I see the judge, attorney for the other side, and their witnesses all showing up in the same car. My attorney tells me I have to accept this tribunal. We can't have it tried before an unbiased Article III judge.

- My lawyer tells me I can't sue the government. They destroyed my business.

The list is not meant to be an all-inclusive list of litigation or personal injury problems, but it is a good start. Let's move on to a brief history leading up to the recent evolution of the expansion of liability.

Chapter 2

The Evolution of Tort Law

A Brief History

Our law for the most part originated in and was carried over from England. Six hundred years ago, the king or queen was the law; the monarch was the chief executive, legislative body, and judiciary all wrapped up in one. He or she hired, paid, and fired the judges if they were displeasing. The monarchy had allowed a parliament to be formed, but only as an advisory board, not a legislative body. The king's or queen's rule was supreme, as there was no higher authority. They were the undisputed sovereigns—there was no higher authority. At that time, it was good to be the monarch, but not so good to be the subjects.

The history of England is the relentless encroaching on this sovereign power from all branches until in England today the monarch has become a mere figurehead. Political power rests with the Parliament—more specifically, the House of Commons. They incrementally pressed for and achieved independence from the king and queen. Today, the final determination of English courts must be approved by Parliament.

When the North American colonies broke away from England, they carried over the North Atlantic many aspects of English judicial and legislative law and procedure, including tort law. However, as the colonies were starting anew, they discarded some undesirable aspects and aspects that simply did not conform to the new colonial order.

The Common Law

After achieving independence from the monarchy, English judges handed down rulings that were consistent with their personal values, limited only by their cognitive skills. However, it became clear that when five or ten judges would rule on the same set of facts, one would really hit the mark better than the others. England is a small country, and judges would get together and discuss cases before them. The inclination of the other judges was to conform their decisions to this superior reasoning and judgment. They would all adopt the ruling that seemed correct or, in some cases, more correct. This consensus gave rise to the common law, in which the principle of a ruling is followed by others as precedent. This was judge-made law, as opposed to legislative acts. Later, these common-law principles were incorporated into legislative acts that prevailed over common law. However, where there is no statute, common law prevails.

As an example, A and B enter into an agreement wherein A agrees to sell his cow to B for one pound. A delivers the cow to B, and B agrees to pay the one pound the following morning. A dies that night. A's son and representative of the estate of A demands the purchase price. B stiffs the son with "Who are you? I entered into a contract with A, and only he can enforce it." There is no privity of contract. This type of problem is given to a number of judges. One judge would get it right by finding the son is a third-party beneficiary of the contract between A and B or, in equity, that B would be unjustly enriched if allowed to keep the cow and not pay for it. When judges get together, they are impressed by the wisdom of this reasoning. This ruling then becomes a principle and part of the common law of England, and later the common law of the United States, and finally a subject of legislative acts.

Statutory Law

This body of law we call the common law was carried over to the colonies essentially intact. However, the legislative body soon began to encroach on this body of case law by replacing it with legislative acts. As this was within the power of the legislature, the common law—where inconsistent with a legislative act—had to be subservient to statutory law. This is subject to constitutional restraints and, ultimately, the voting booth. When I practiced law, 1962 to 1997, I was witness to virtually the last vestiges of common law being replaced by federal and state statutory law. Today, seldom do you find a suit being determined by common law.

Today, law is established first by the Constitution and then by legislative acts, both modified at times by case law under the banner of interpretation. In the United States, we give great deference to our court decisions. This is inherently part of our separation of powers doctrine set forth in Articles I, II, and III of our Constitution. Our problems today are in part the result of our blurring the constitutionally imposed distinction among legislative, executive, and judicial powers.

At the federal level, our legislative body complains but tolerates our executive and judiciary legislating. Congress is hardly in a position to complain; it has delegated legislative power to the other two branches of government and to its own regulators. This is more fully developed in chapter 5, about administrative law courts, where overreaching and abuses of power are shown to occur. Congress has legislative powers it can employ to protect its interests and curtail these abuses but has not done so. Compare this mind-set with Great Britain's House of Commons, which seems to delight in undoing judicial determinations by legislation.

Instead, here, unhappy legislative losers have adopted the practice of dumping legislative matters before our Supreme Court, then complaining when the court legislates or determines the matter against them. In some cases, the judiciary refuses to rule on the matter, deeming it nonjusticiable—in other words, it is a legislative issue, not a judicial issue. Therefore Congress, not the courts, should decide the issue. Our courts justify their judicial restraint upon the grounds they are restricted by our Constitution and the doctrine of separation of powers.

Instead of recapturing its delegated legislative power, our Congress devotes their attention to relentlessly infringing on an easier target, namely state legislative matters, amassing powers previously held by the states. This transfer of political and economic power from the states to the federal government was not what our founders had in mind. Our Constitution clearly delineates the limited powers we give the federal government in Article I, Section 8. To drive the point home, our Tenth Amendment provides that all powers not delegated to Congress are reserved to the states or to the people. We bear witness how well recent deviations from these provisions have worked out.

As we have decided it is our legislative branch that determines what is tortious and what is not, what is lawful and what is not, it is of great importance to the citizen exactly who is making the above distinctions, as it determines whether you have a cause of action or whether you have a defense. In summary, we have a separation of powers problem as well as a federalism problem, but our branches of government seem uninterested in solving the very problems they created.

Introduction to Evolution of Extended Liability

The foundation of recovery was originally based upon negligence defined as: (a) a legal duty to use due care, (b) a breach of that duty, and (c) that breech being the proximate or legal cause of the resulting injury.

When we attempt to impose reasonable parameters on the duty, we start with the holding in *Palsgraf v. Long Island R. Co.* (1928) 248 N. York. Simplified, Palsgraf held that behavior is negligent when it creates an unreasonable risk of harm to some general class of people. The scope of the duty places a restriction on liability to anybody outside the class. Stated differently, liability of unforeseeable consequences is avoided by limiting the scope of the duty, as opposed to simply saying defendant's conduct was not the proximate cause of the plaintiff's injury. In addition, an intervening cause may well be another limitation on the scope of liability.

To establish some semblance of stability and certainty, the American Law Institute has published *A Concise Restatement of Torts*, covering torts as well as other areas of the law. We are now into the third edition.

Restatements attempt to give the general consensus of judicial and legislative determinations. The restatements of the law are looked on and cited as authority—persuasive authority.

The *Restatement of Torts*, part 3, section 3, provides the primary inquiry still is whether the defendant should have acted with reasonable care, if the defendant failed to exercise reasonable care, and if the plaintiff's injury was the proximate or legal result of the defendant's behavior.

The *Restatement of Torts*, part 3, section 8, provides that the above elements are factual issues for the trier of facts to determine. However, if there is no evidence on one side or the other, the judge may step in and determine the issue. In fact, the judge has a duty to do so, even when a jury has reached the unsupportable conclusion.

The application of the requirement of a duty owed to a specific class and proximate cause has serious drawbacks if you are of the mind-set that no person injured by some act of another should be sent from our courts empty-handed. This belief conflicts with traditional approaches that required the plaintiff's factual situations fit within the structure of tort law. Failing to do so resulted in being sent home without a recovery.

Three figures come to mind when searching for leaders in changes in the law of torts: William Prosser, University of California, Berkeley; California Supreme Court Chief Justice Roger Trainer; and Professor John D. Wade,

Vanderbilt University. These three men, along with other visionaries, framed changes in the law of liability for tortious behavior, first through writings, then through court decisions, and finally through "me too" legislative acts. Let us go through some of these changes.

In the field of torts, there is a class of people who are the consumers of goods. Two hundred years ago, we had simpler times with simple solutions to problems surrounding the purchase and sale of goods. However, with industrialization and technology, matters became infinitely more complicated. Today, if an automobile causes personal injury to the plaintiff, the plaintiff is hard-pressed to ascertain whether the designer, the manufacturer, the wholesaler, the retailer, or the guy who put the tires on the car is the culprit. The complexity of today's automobile defies easy ascertainment of the exact cause resulting in injury to the plaintiff.

This has given rise to an endless expansion of problems associated with the purchase of goods. One increasingly common aspect is that the seller has more knowledge of the product than the purchaser. You, as the buyer, could have been expected to grasp what made a buggy go, but today, not a modern car. You could have taken an older telephone apart to see how it functioned, but not a smartphone.

This disparity, if unchecked, can result in great injustices as sellers have an opportunity take advantage of buyers. If buyers were relegated to negligence and fault as the criterion, many a plaintiff would go home empty-handed.

Visionaries sought to level the playing field. Out of this emerged changes in tort law.

Res Ipsa Loquitur

One class of injured plaintiffs received injuries but understandably did not know and could not have been expected to know who was at fault. For example, the doctor, after being told by her patient that he has pain and discomfort in the abdomen, advises her patient he will need an exploratory operation. The patient checks into the hospital, is prepared for the procedure, and is wheeled into the operating room, prepared, and put under. He awakes later having the same symptoms as before. He is assured by the operating doctor and staff that the pain and discomfort will go away as his body heals. They don't.

Three weeks later he returns to his doctor to find out why his condition has not improved. He is told he must check in to the hospital where they will cut him open again and see what is going on. He complies. Upon cutting him open a second time, they find a sponge has been left in his abdomen.

Our patient—now plaintiff—has been hurt, and somebody is responsible for leaving the sponge in, but he does not know who and cannot reasonably be expected to know who the real defendant is. He is confronted with a wall of silence. The operating doctor and the postoperation doctor are not talking. The nurses are not talking; the hospital staff is not talking. The patient is at a loss as to who the defendant is.

Our visionaries stepped in with a solution by changing the burden of proof. Normally, each element of a cause of action must be proven by the plaintiff. Clearly, under the circumstances, he cannot do so. But under the doctrine of res ipsa loquitur, he is only required to prove what he knows—that is, in this case: "I checked in to the hospital; they wheeled me into the operating room and put me under. I know I later woke up with the same pain and discomfort. I again checked in to the hospital. They opened me up and found a sponge."

At that point, the burden of proof changes. Upon establishing these foundational facts, there arises a presumption that somebody in that operating room was negligent in failing to remove the sponge. This presumption will carry the issue as to each target defendant, unless rebutted by substantive admissible evidence to the contrary. Therefore, there arises an obligation for each target defendant to come forward and establish he or she was not the negligent defendant. Self-interest encourages all to come forward with a disclosure of the facts. If a trial is a search for the truth, this doctrine advances this cause.

Understandably, there is need to prevent plaintiffs who have equal access to the facts from attempting to use this doctrine to shift the burden of proof. Their foundational facts must demonstrate the need to apply the doctrine.

Warranties

EXPRESS WARRANTIES

An express warranty is little more than making producers
and sellers of goods make good on their promises or representations concerning the products they sell. If they say
the product will do something, it must be able to do it, or
they must respond to the consumer who is damaged by the
failure of the product to do what they said it would do. This
doctrine is part contract and part tort. It makes each promise or representation part of the agreement of purchase and
sale, regardless of whether it was part of an oral or written
contract. The only issue is whether the misrepresentation
caused the injury or damage. This doctrine has morphed
into what is found in our present *Restatement of Torts*, 3rd
edition, chapter 16, section 9: "fraudulent, *negligent* or *innocent* representation of a material fact" is the basis for
imposing liability if that misrepresentation causes injury.

IMPLIED WARRANTIES

Our courts can imply the seller's representation or misrepresentation in more than one way. People who sell, noting
the exposure when they make clear open representations
regarding their product, find ways to create the same impression indirectly by inference and innuendo. A multi-
billion-dollar industry surrounds the peddling of creams,
lotions, scented dust particles, and slabs of plaster coverings

that cosmetics users slather on. But first these companies must create insecurity and uncertainty in the prospective buyer. The merchandiser must create the impression in the perspective buyer, "You're getting old, ugly, and undesirable." They then trot out a twenty-year-old with flawless skin before the viewer with the not-so-subtle suggestion, "You can again look like this if you will buy the product." Sadly, consumers bite, and the industry flourishes.

When the buyer later determines that the product will not peel back the years, and she seeks redress, the seller quickly points out, "We didn't tell her she would return to the face of a twenty-year-old." This is where the judicial system steps in and cuts through the fluff. Our courts can imply that what the peddler suggests indirectly is in fact an outright representation and treat the seller in the same manner as the "express promisor." In short, the seller implied; therefore, the seller must make good if the product fails to meet the buyer's reasonable expectations that the seller fostered.

A second implied warranty is the warranty that the product is of merchantable quality. Merchantable establishes a standard and that the product, if reasonably used in the manner intended, will do what it is supposed to do.

The Restatement of Torts, *3rd Edition, Weighs In*
The *Restatement of Torts* has attempted to cut through much of the traditional, somewhat formalistic approach and simplify the overall approach.

Chapter 16, section A2(1), provides: "One engaged in the business of selling or otherwise distributing product, who sells or distributes a defective product is subject to liability for harm to persons or property caused by the defect."

Chapter 16, section A(2), paraphrased, provides there are three classes of defects. The product may have a manufacturing defect, it may have a design defect, or the seller may have failed to give adequate instructions so that "the foreseeable risks of harm posed by the product could have been reduced or avoided. The omission of the instructions or warnings renders the product not reasonably safe."

Chapter 16, section 18, provides the seller cannot escape liability for a defective product by incorporating into the sale agreement disclaimers, limitations, waivers, or other exculpatory clauses.

Chapter 16, section 17, provides for "comparative negligence." If the plaintiff contributes to the injury, or is partially at fault, the award to any and all defendants is apportioned. There are still jurisdictions where evidence of the plaintiff's fault is inadmissible, but most states adopt comparative negligence between plaintiff and defendants as well as between defendants.

This law has been applied to grinding wheels, high-speed printing presses, champagne bottles, and battery-operated imitation cigarettes. The court takes into consideration factors such as consumer expectations and whether the consumer can even intelligently inspect the goods for defects.

Even a product that has open or obvious problems does not preclude recovery for damages if the plaintiff can establish there was a safer alternative for the manufacturer. The defense of assumption of the risk gives way to the manufacturer's obligation to put products on the market free of defects in manufacturing, defects, or design.

This present law provides a check on the manufacturer and distributor. But in addition, federal and state agencies such as the Occupational Safety and Health Administration (OSHA) and the countless regulations thereunder have produced laws protecting, and at times overprotecting, the consumer. Finally, the tort lawyer is a further check, as manufacturers and distributors do not want to spend their time and resources in a courtroom.

Strict Liability in Tort

In the natural sequence of expansive events, it was only a matter of time before our courts found a way to completely sidestep plaintiffs' traditional requirement of some showing of negligence, intentional tort, or recovery upon warranty associated with a sale and purchase of goods. Strict liability in tort was formulated by the visionaries previously identified and adopted by our courts, led by Roger Trainer, chief justice of the California Supreme Court.

In my last year in law school, I was exposed to the first case imposing strict liability; this was imposed on Cutter Labs. In the first Cutter Labs case, the court was confronted with the harshest of facts, presenting an incredibly difficult issue.

Jonas Salk and others developed a vaccine that cured polio. Cutter Labs was one of the producers of this drug. Millions were injected with this drug with outstanding results. The drug was looked on as a godsend.

However, in this early stage of endless litigation, a handful of recipients had horrible reactions to the drug administered to them. People were paralyzed and some died. What made this case so difficult was the fact that millions took the vaccine without repercussions. The drug was of great social benefit to millions, so there was no way the courts or the legislative body would intervene or permanently prohibit the administration of the drug.

There was no evidence of negligence. The injuring doses were identical to the millions of doses that had benefited others without repercussions. There was also no evidence that the doses in question were defective, nor did they deviate from the other administered drugs in any manner, thus eliminating warranty. In short, there were no facts warranting application of the traditional measures of negligence or warranty, and yet a small number of people were injured when the drug was administered.

The California appellate and supreme courts put together a decision allowing recovery against Cutter Labs using the following reasoning: First, the drug was inherently dangerous. The administering of the drug gave rise to a risk of loss. Second, the consumers were not in a position to protect themselves by inspection.

The question, therefore, was, who should bear this risk of loss? The court then launched into a new consideration. They determined this was an insurable risk—just pay the premium, and the insurance company will bear the burden when the loss is incurred, thereby spreading the loss among everybody, reflected in premium cost. They then determined that the seller of the drug was better suited to carry insurance to cover the loss. So, in effect, the loss would be spread about so nobody had to bear the full burden. It would not be practical to have everybody buy an individual insurance policy to protect against this risk of loss. The insurance company, when paying for the loss, would simply increase its insurance premium. Assuming the risk is an expense of doing business.

Strict liability in tort is the result. Swept aside are traditional measures of liability. The burden on plaintiff tort lawyers was dramatically altered. The issue burden now would be to successfully characterize goods or products that injure a client as "inherently dangerous."

One can understand why a drug that triggers a violent reaction in one's immune system may be considered inherently dangerous. However, the reasoning behind the Cutter Labs decision has opened the door to endless tort litigation. An expert on the witness stand could with a straight face characterize the common pencil as inherently dangerous, as one could poke oneself in the eye.

After this case was decided, many more people reacted adversely to the drug, rendering the initial decision questionable, but the reasoning of the court remains with us. The court now takes into consideration whether one party or the other, as a practical matter, can insure against the risk of loss. This results in a windfall to insurance companies with an explosion of policies, policies demanded by sellers as a defense against being wiped out with one lawsuit that goes badly.

This theory of recovery was fleshed out by the California Supreme Court in *Greenman v. Yuba Power Products* 59 Cal. 2, on page 62: "A manufacturer is strictly liable in tort when an article he places on the market, knowing that it is to be used without inspection for defects, proves to have defect that causes injury to a human being." Thus, there is no need to rely on warranty.

The court followed, explaining that while these cases originally sounded in contract and breach of warranty, this liability was imposed by law, not by a contractual relationship. The manufacturer's liability was imposed by law; therefore, the court would not permit the manufacturer to define the scope of his liability. The court stated:

> The purpose of such liability is to ensure that the costs of injuries resulting from defective products

are borne by the manufacturer that put the products on the market rather than by the injured persons who are powerless to protect themselves. Sale warranties serve this purpose fitfully at best.

The *Restatement of Torts*, 3rd edition, chapter 15, section 20, approaches the problem this way:

(a) An actor who carries on an abnormally dangerous activity is subject to strict liability for physical harm resulting from the activity.

(b) An activity is abnormally dangerous if: (1) the activity creates a foreseeable and highly significant risk of physical harm even when reasonable care is exercised by all actors; and (2) the activity is not one of common usage.

In summary, the requirements of negligence and intentional tort are swept aside; express or implied warranty pose no problem to the plaintiff. Our courts first and now our legislatures visit liability for inherently dangerous activity, if foreseeable, even though of great benefit to society. If you are a manufacturer of these goods, "wrong" has been taken out of the definition of tort. It is with this historical background that I discuss the following problems.

Chapter 3

The Problems

Generally speaking, we have problems with the administration of our tort, or personal injury, system now in
place—some serious, some not. The system's function and
primary purpose is to justly compensate injured plaintiffs
and resolve differences between people and their government. In the personal injury arena, we look for facts that
support the conclusion that the plaintiff had a right and
the defendant had a duty owed to the plaintiff, that the
defendant breached that duty, that the defendant's breach
was the proximate cause of injury to the plaintiff, and that
the plaintiff was in fact injured. It is in the best interests of
both the plaintiff and the defendant to expediently reach
this determination one way or the other.

Complicating matters, with the growth of government, its laws and regulations, we increasingly create

controversies between the governing force and the governed. We inevitably must deal with government's scope of authority versus the individual's rights. The courtroom is the arena where we seek out the truth and resolve these differences.

There are obstacles to achieving that goal. First, achieving that goal is made far more difficult when we have many hands in the cookie jar. Second, we have problems with consistency and with predictability of result. In an ideal world, the attorney should be able to ascertain the expected result after uncovering the facts that control the case. After applying the law, the attorney should be able to go to his client and opposing counsel and work out an equitable settlement of the dispute. Sadly, this is not always the case.

Third, we have adopted the adversarial system, as opposed to the inquisitorial system. In the adversarial system, we assume that if each party to a suit appears—independently, with or without counsel—and advances his or her own cause, we are likely to reach a just result. As a further check, we have a limited right to have a jury of our peers determine all factual issues. The judge's role is more like that of a neutral arbitrator whose role is to keep things fair—that is, to ensure all parties have an opportunity to present relevant and material evidence.

However, many Western European nations adopt the inquisitorial system, where the judge takes a more active role. It is the judge who poses questions to the witnesses, and in most cases, the judge replaces the jury in the fact-finding role.

From this setting, problems emerge, as defined in the introduction. Let's start with the first.

It Takes Too Long

The Background

We must start by acknowledging there are more cases filed each year; however, there are more judges appointed each year and more courtrooms built. And this does not explain why we have too many dark, empty courtrooms, day after day. We have a problem in that when the parties finally get their trial date, the court administrator will set aside a judge, bailiff, court reporter, clerk, and most importantly, the courtroom. Then the parties engage in mutual blustering but settle the case on the eve of trial. There is no practical way another case can be substituted in at the last minute—the potential substitute parties are not ready; therefore, the courtroom is vacant for the week.

The parties will engage in bluffing, demanding a jury trial when they intend to waive a jury at the last minute. However, the demand of a jury extends the trial one day, perhaps two, and this extended period is set aside. Stated differently, the parties demand five days when they have evidence for two, perhaps three days. A timelier candid assessment would allow the court administrator to fit in another two- or three-day matter.

There is desperation in parties who find themselves waiting for a courtroom, particularly when a statutory limitation is on the horizon. Lawyers for both sides have been known to find a dispute that is close to settling; however, it is set for an early date. The early trial date is important enough so the parties at the end of the line have been known to come up with the money necessary to settle the earlier case if they can have the earlier time slot. Judges look favorably on such arrangements as they promote settlement and shorten the trial calendar.

Another time consumer is trial judges are called upon to also handle law and motion matters. This cuts into the time remaining for actual trial. Wherever possible, a single judge should be given the law and motion calendar, freeing the others for trial work.

A trial day starting at 8:00 a.m. is rare; 10:00 a.m. is more like it. After an hour off for lunch, the question is how long the trial day will go in the afternoon. The judge often settles on 3:00 p.m., so everybody can prepare for tomorrow. The bottom line is that people spend about four hours a day in trial.

Trial Work Is Tough—Get It Over With

That said, it has been my experience that some judges run a tight, efficient trial calendar. In a criminal tax evasion case, where I represented the defendant, the federal district court judge advised counsel on Monday that the case would conclude that week, even if the parties had to put in eight-hour days and work on Sunday after church. We concluded trial Friday afternoon.

In another of my cases, dealing with fraud and concealment under the Securities Exchange Act 1933-34 Rule 10(b)(5), the same admonition was given on Monday: that the judge would be commencing his next case on the following Monday, that the parties should be prepared to work until 9:00 p.m. and start at 8:00 a.m., and that we would work Saturday and Sunday if necessary. We concluded that trial Saturday morning. Unfortunately, these personal examples are the exceptions, not the rule.

Continuances

Continuances, if freely granted, leave courtrooms empty. They also make it more difficult for the trier of facts to stay on top of the litigation as memories fade. I have been exposed to a trial where nine continuances were granted, four in the middle of trial. The result: each time, the courtroom went dark. Additionally, this trial tactic was brutal in that the defendant attorneys seeking the continuances were local, while I lived and worked on the other side of the state and had to make repeated long-distance trips to the courtroom.

There is no question that this tactic, sanctioned by the local judge, was designed to make it financially impractical to continue pursuing the cause of action. Had it been successful, the defendant's counsel would have successfully concluded the lawsuit on grounds other than its merits.

The point here is that we are not using our courtroom time and judges wisely. Trial judges should take better control over their calendars. There must be a good, credible reason before continuances are granted. Counsel moving for a continuance should be ready to give good reason that should prevail over the obvious injury to the responding party. Also, the moving party must satisfy the judge that this is not a tactic, the result of which would be to squander valuable court time.

In line with the preceding, I have been subjected to endless motions by large law firms with deep pockets seeking to bury their opposition with endless options, with the expectation of driving the opposition into the ground. Each mindless motion devours court time and resources.

The immediate remedy that comes to mind is for the judge to impose sanctions on the offending party, awarding to the injured party reasonable attorney fees and costs, defending against such tactics.

Remedial Measures

As a remedial measure, states have enacted statutes that require the plaintiff, after filing a complaint, to get the matter to trial within a specific period. As an example, California has a three-year discretionary and five-year mandatory dismissal statute. If the plaintiff fails to get the matter to trial within five years, the defendant can move to dismiss the case. However, this effort on the part of the legislature to move matters along has drawbacks. It opens the door to defendants adopting shabby trial tactics such as evading service for two or three years, then delaying discovery, filing endless demurrers, motions to strike, and motions for summary judgment until the statutory period has run out. The defendant then moves to have the case dismissed under the mandatory limitation statute. While the practice is disingenuous, at times it takes place.

Each of the above items significantly contributes to the legitimate complaint that the process takes too long.

It Is Too Expensive

There are multiple reasons why litigation is expensive, none pleasant. We simply have too many people or corporations with their hands in the cookie jar. They have to be satisfied before the litigation can be settled. I say settled because 90 percent of claims are eventually settled as opposed to going to trial.

The Ethical Problem

The following example is not intended to cast all lawyers in a bad light but to illustrate the problem. I filed a complaint on behalf of an unpaid subcontractor against the contractor who failed make the last payment on the contract, wherein the subcontractor had agreed to install a metal roof on commercial buildings at a ski resort, per plans and specifications. The contractor had agreed to pay a specific price in five installments. After the job was satisfactorily completed and accepted, the contractor refused to make the last payment. The plaintiff's first count was to recover this payment. A second count was filed against the owner to foreclose on a mechanics lien.

The resort in question is located at around six thousand feet in elevation and receives a great deal of snow each winter. This snow melts during the day and then freezes at night. The accumulated snow melts when warmed by the roof, which is heated from below, but does not melt where the roof overhangs the building.

This is an invitation for future disaster unless you keep the snow, which turns to ice, from building up. As water melts during the day on the roof adjacent to the portion warmed by the heat in the building, it is stopped by an ice dam that forms around the overhang. The ice dam builds up until water running off the roof backs up to where it runs down the inside walls. Not good.

Additionally, the architect who designed the buildings wanted them to look like a quaint replica of buildings in the Swiss Alps, so he designed little crickets, or dormers, each breaking the roof envelope and continuity of the slope, and each adding to the formation of ice dams.

This problem was known by and discussed by the roofer, his contractor, and the owner prior to installation. The solution to the potential problem was keeping snow off the roof and, more importantly, breaking up any forming ice dams. The owner performed no maintenance, so when winter hit, the snow fell and ice dams began to form. During the first winter that ice dams formed, water cascaded down the interior walls.

The simple lawsuit by the subcontractor to recover the last installment was soon buried by one cross-complaint after another, some cross-complaints sounding in tort and warranty (still a tort). This resulted in five separate sets of attorneys, each pointing fingers at other parties. Also, these attorneys—other than me, representing the subcontractor—represented the parties but were selected and paid for by insurance companies that had been dragged into the suit.

Once an insurance company receives a claim and hires a law firm, it sets aside a certain amount of money for the claim against its insured. Attorneys working for an insurance company but representing a party to the action are confronted with an ethical conundrum. If the attorney works to settle the lawsuit or try it quickly and expediently, he serves his client of record and the insurance company who hired him. If he strings out the suit with endless depositions, interrogatories, and motions to produce, he can eat up the reserve in attorney fees, leaving a sufficient amount to settle the suit when the time to settle arrives.

To add to the ethical problem, these lawyers meet with each other time and time again in court. Some socialize with their opponents' lawyers. While the social connection may well be innocent, it raises the eyebrows of their respective clients. It blurs the adversarial system we take pride in.

In defense of the practice, a malpractice lawsuit may hinge on a deposition not taken or interrogatories not lodged; therefore, a degree of justification is found in fear of omission. It stretches credulity to believe the insurance company is not aware of the preceding practice. The consumption of the reserve simply becomes a cost of doing business, to be reflected in the next premium. In this case, depositions were repeatedly taken of the same witnesses; the same questions were asked and the same answers given.

The bottom line is that the purpose of a suit is to return the plaintiff and cross-complainants to the financial position they were in before the contract breach or tortious act of the defendants. If the party is insured, this is not the purpose for which the insured pays the insurance company premiums.

The above practice is expensive to the client and does not further that person's cause. Additionally, the attorney is confronted with the unsolvable dilemma of balancing two conflicting goals: resolving the dispute expediently and keeping the malpractice lawyer away.

The Good Old Days Are Gone

When I started practicing law, rural judges had one secretary each. If two lawyers felt the case should be settled, the common practice was to call the judge's secretary, who would arrange a settlement conference. In many cases, the attorneys would walk out of the judge's chambers two hours later having settled the suit. In some cases, the judge, after reviewing the file and sensing the case would settle, would call the attorneys in for a settlement conference. In either case, the matter would be disposed of at minimal cost to the clients and relieve the court's calendar of one more case.

Not so today. Today, standing in the way, we have a court administrator who has an assistant, and both have secretaries. Attorneys are required to contact the administrator, not the judges or their secretaries. Another stage, or level, of bureaucracy has intervened. The administrator will evaluate the situation and determine when, if at all, a person can see the judge. Lawyers are buried in a bureaucratic process when this access decision would be much better handled by the judge or the judge's secretary. The point is that this makes it immeasurably more difficult to settle a case with the help of the judge. It also erects a needless obstacle to effective representation of clients.

The financial expectations of law students going into practice bear little resemblance to my expectations when I started practice. I was taken into an office with a $250 monthly retainer and 50 percent of what I made beyond that amount. That was all I could expect, and I am not sure I was worth it, as a seasoned secretary was far more valuable.

Less than twenty years later, the expectation of a law student going into practice in an urban area could be $100,000 a year. After all, that lawyer would have to have enough to make payments on his Mercedes-Benz, his spouse's BMW, and his $400,000 home. These expectations, if met, require an enormous amount of billable time at a rate far exceeding the attorney's worth to the firm or to the client he is working for. Notwithstanding, this cost is passed on to the client.

As firms mature, the founders no longer want to try cases. Golf is far more pleasant. They show up and drag in clients but leave the work to others. This increases the amount the firm must charge to support everybody, not just those who draft papers or go to court. This is also reflected in the bill to the client. This, in part, explains why litigation is so expensive.

Expensive Trial Tactics

Large law firms delight in running the opposing single practitioner into the ground by filing endless repeated motions, demurrers, and other pleadings and presenting the same issues previously decided over and over again. The modus operandi is initiated by one set of lawyers preparing the endless chain of motions, a second set filing each motion and obtaining an order shortening time to the following day, and a third set appearing and arguing the motion. While this practice may be enjoyable for the large firm, it is oppressive to single practitioners and their clients. Somebody has to pay for all this.

In more than one case during trial, I, as a single trial practitioner, was repeatedly served with a copy of a motion for judgment on the pleadings or for summary judgment, together with an order shortening time. I was expected after the trial day to prepare opposition to the motion, including affidavits, declarations, and points and authorities, and to have them ready by 8:00 a.m. the following day.

During this period, the single practitioner is also supposed to prepare for trial resuming at 10:00 a.m. The objective of this practice is to force the single practitioner to cave in, thus disposing of litigation on grounds other than its merits.

The impact of this practice is to make litigation more expensive for both the single practitioner and the well-heeled large firm relentlessly pursuing this trial tactic. There are needless costs involved with the preparation of the motion, the response to the motion, the appearances of both sides, and finally the mindless consumption of judge and court time.

The immediate remedy for the most part lies with the judge hearing the matter, who, sensing the trial tactic, can and should impose financial sanctions on the offending party. The party initiating the trial tactic is evidencing an ethical problem.

Hopefully, the preceding, while not excusing the high cost of litigation, sets forth some of the reasons for it.

Joint and Several Liability

Legislators have options in establishing rules for imposing liability on joint feasors. Legislators may elect to visit joint liability on all defendants, several liability on each defendant, or joint and several liability. If you as a defendant are jointly liable, you are liable for the full amount of the judgment even though you are at best a marginal defendant having little to do with the incident that gave rise to the litigation. If you are severally or proportionately liable, you are liable only for the damage you caused. Stated differently, you are not liable for the portion of liability other defendants may have caused. If you are jointly and severally liable, the law allows the plaintiff to go after all defendants for the whole of the judgment. The law then allows the defendants to sort out the proportion of liabilities attributable to each.

Most states have elected to go with joint and several liability, so my discussion concentrates on that alternative. The plaintiffs' bar argues that joint or joint and several is the proper alternative, as defendants are in the best position to sort out their respective liabilities. Let the plaintiff put on a case and achieve a full judgment. The plaintiff then does not have to expend more resources pursuing the lawsuit and assuming the obligation to establish proportionate responsibility of each defendant.

The plaintiff obtains another advantage. If a major tortfeasor has no money, the plaintiff can then proceed against the deep pockets for that bankrupt defendant's share of responsibility. The bottom line is that the law makes sure the plaintiff is fully compensated, even though the deep-pockets defendant is required to come up with more than a proportionate share. This underlying principle is advanced with the argument that without joint liability, plaintiff's counsel would be discouraged from taking a case, not because there is no merit in the claim but because neither the lawyer nor the client will receive compensation.

This fits into the social philosophy that every injured person should have a day in court. The opposition argues this encourages plaintiffs' lawyers to beat the bushes for someone with deep pockets as opposed to attempting to find who is at fault. All you need is to establish 1 percent or so proportionate liability, and then Deep Pockets is on the hook if the major tortfeasor proves judgment-proof.

The deeper issue in these cases is whether it is more important to ensure the plaintiff receives full compensation or that defendants should only be responsible for the injury they caused. This pits two philosophical principles against each other. The first is the conviction that one who has been injured by another is entitled to be fully compensated. We legislatively manifest support for this principle when we expand tort liability with the doctrine of res ipsa loquitur, warranties, and strict liability in tort.

When under the second principle we allow a plaintiff to recover in full against a deep-pockets defendant who is at best marginally responsible, we are taking from one and giving to another without any semblance of due process of law. The question we must ask is which principle should prevail. Right or wrong, the trend of our legislatures and courts is to fully compensate one who has been injured by others. So, realistically, it is not likely any legislative tort reform will be forthcoming.

Contribution

Some states have attempted to alleviate the harshness of joint liability. California's Civil Code of Procedure, section 875(a), has provided a right of contribution between two or more tortfeasors. Essentially, it provides that when one defendant ends up paying more than a proportionate share of a judgment, other defendants may be required to contribute. Understandably, there are limitations. The willful wrongdoer is not entitled to contribution. The right of contribution applies only when there is a joint judgment. In ascertaining the ultimate liability of each joint tortfeasor, the court looks to and attempts to apply equitable principles.

Insurance companies may avail themselves of the right of subrogation when they acquire the standing of the insured tortfeasor after paying off a portion of somebody else's liability. The *Restatement of Torts*, 3rd edition, section C(23), concurs but adds you cannot recover any amount in excess the amount you actually paid in excess of the primary tortfeasor's pro rata share. If you have the right of indemnity, you cannot exercise your right of contribution.

Indemnity

If in a joint liability state you have joint liability, but in your case there is a distinction between one who is primarily liable and another who is secondarily liable, a right of indemnity arises; the tortfeasor who is secondarily liable has a right of indemnity against the primary defendant. Secondarily means "without active fault," that is, fault that is imputed or constructive. As an example, the defendant employer of the defendant truck driver who caused an accident is secondarily liable; the *Restatement of Torts*, section C(22), concurs. The right of indemnity hinges on proving your liability was vicarious, not direct, or that you are the seller of a defective product and are not independently culpable—that is, you didn't know the product was defective.

We must distinguish between indemnity, where you recover your pro rata share, and contribution, where liability is visited equally. Both are efforts by the legislator to lessen the impact of the harshness that results from taking from a joint feasor more than their allocate share of liability.

The Collateral Source Rule

The collateral source rule in *Helfend v. Southern Cal. Rapid Transit Dist.* 2 Cal. 3d 1, 6 (1970) provides: "In an action against the wrongdoer for the damages suffered is not precluded nor is the amount of the damages reduced by the receipt by him of payment for his loss from a source wholly independent of the wrongdoer."

In short, if you are a defendant or a defendant's lawyer in a tort action, you cannot introduce evidence that the plaintiff has been or will be wholly or partially compensated for the loss. This rule has been embraced by many jurisdictions. See the *Restatement of Torts*, 3rd edition, section 920A(2). The *Restatement* states that this includes benefits to the injured plaintiff from: insurance the plaintiff has paid for, employment benefits received, gratuities, or social legislation benefits.

While many theories have been advanced supporting this principle, in essence, the court looks on the collateral source rule as preventing the wrongdoers from gaining a windfall by having someone else pay part of their obligation to make the plaintiff whole. This can be stated differently: the court looks on the defendants as having been unjustly enriched. Why? Because they have not been compelled to pay the full amount of the damages.

I take issue with this reasoning. This is a civil, not a criminal, proceeding. The purpose of tort law is to make a plaintiff whole, not punish the defendant. When insurance is involved, the waters are muddied. One could argue that if the plaintiff is covered by the incident, the plaintiff should be awarded the cost of the plaintiff's premium.

The question to ask, by this reasoning, is this: if the defendant, not the plaintiff, secures insurance coverage, is the defendant not unjustly enriched when the insurance company pays off? Understandably, we recognize this is a contract obligation the defendant's insurance has paid for. So courts have yet to go that far, as we recognize the defendant has paid for that insurance by paying insurance premiums. The insurance company is simply upholding its end of the bargain. In summary, there is therefore something wrong with the court's reasoning. The civil court judge is imposing punishment as compensation. If the court wants to impose punishment, punitive damages are the appropriate remedy.

But under the collateral source rule, reduced to its fundamentals, the majority of courts have decided to allow the plaintiff to recover 150 percent, as opposed to the defendant only having to pay 50 percent. This reasoning would hold water if tort actions were only premised on intentional or negligent behavior. But realistically we already have expanded liability to the point where much of the liability is visited on the defendant without consideration of wrongful behavior.

Another argument is made, namely that the introduction of this evidence will confuse the jury, and then there will be an inclination on the jury's part to reduce the award by the amount received from another source. The argument is premised upon the suspicion that a jury properly instructed on the law will choose to ignore the admonishment to disregard the collateral source evidence.

There is irony in this position. We cherish the institution we call the jury. By our Constitution and supporting legislation, parties in civil and criminal courts have a right to a jury trial. Our courts of appeal give great deference to the final determination of a jury on an issue of fact. But when it comes to the collateral source rule, we paternalistically exclude relevant evidence on the issue of a plaintiff's damages, or actual loss. We justify this by contending the jury just won't understand and, therefore, will not follow the law.

A response to this dilemma is to have certain complex trials administered by those who have the expertise to digest the "confusing" evidence. Understandably, there is pushback from those who argue the party is entitled to a "jury of his or her peers," not a panel of experts selected by others. This discussion is developed more fully in the summary and conclusions.

A separate justification for the collateral source rule lies with the court's noting that the plaintiff never obtains full compensation, as the plaintiff's attorney gets part of the award, thereby reducing the net recovery. The answer to that contention is to handle it directly, by allowing the plaintiff to recover reasonable attorney fees, if successful. However, in fairness, we should allow the defendant attorney fees, if the defendant prevails. Swept aside is the argument that the court is picking and choosing winners and losers.

The counterargument is that we allow the injured plaintiff to not only be fully compensated but recover an amount in excess of actual damages. If a fully compensated plaintiff is the goal, the objective of tort law is taking from the defendant and giving to the plaintiff by making the defendant pay an amount in excess that necessary to make plaintiff whole.

However, the rule is strongly entrenched and is not likely to be altered by tort reform, absent court intervention or legislative change. The drift of the courts as stated above is clear, and this issue will not work its way to the top of the legislature's agenda.

Punitive Damages versus Compensatory Damages

We as a plaintiff have a right to go into court to seek redress for damages caused by a defendant's conduct. We have a right, and a defendant has a duty owed to a plaintiff, which that defendant violated. We are awarded compensatory damages including work loss, actual medical expenses, soft tissue injuries, and mental distress.

So far, so good. The plaintiff is made whole with an award of compensatory damages. However, in most jurisdictions, courts or juries can award punitive damages in addition to compensatory damages. The purpose of an award of punitive damages "is to punish wrongdoers and deter wrongful conduct," as stated in the *Restatement of Torts*, 3rd edition, section 901(c).

Until recently, there was no cap or restraint placed on this amount. This resulted in awards to plaintiffs such as $2,000 compensatory and $2 million in punitive damages. Something went wrong. Unless a defendant was a large corporation or loaded with liability insurance, that defendant was out of business or burdened with a debt that could never be discharged. It is difficult to see any meaningful benefit to society resulting from this legislatively created draconian measure.

There is another problem. If punitive damages are to punish the defendant for conduct, preventing that person from doing it again and deterring others from engaging in this type of conduct, where is the logic in awarding this sum to the plaintiff as opposed to society or perhaps the court that facilitated the suit that gave rise to the award? The whole purpose of tort law and recovery is to put plaintiffs back in the position they were in before injury; it is not, as the *Restatement of Torts*, 3rd edition, section 901(a), explains, to financially destroy defendants.

The next problem is there is no definitive measure of when a defendant's conduct warrants punitive damages. The *Restatement of Torts*, 3rd edition, section 908, allows a punitive damage "for conduct that is outrageous because of the defendant's evil motive or his reckless indifference to the rights of others…" How do you meaningfully explain that to a jury through instructions? What are the guidelines to follow in assessing those issues and then ascertaining the amount to be awarded?

Just what is "outrageous behavior," "evil motive," or "reckless indifference to the rights of others"? Judges are reluctant to place a restraint, depriving a plaintiff of a shot at jackpot justice, resulting in possible grounds for reversal on appeal. Letting the jury decide is a safer path for the judge to take, shoveling the decision-making process onto a jury. The decision will not be upset on appeal unless there is no substantive evidence to support it. Great deference will be given to the jury's determination. The United States Supreme Court has decided punitive damages are a factual issue for the jury to decide. This places the trial judge on the sidelines unless there is no substantial evidence to support the jury's decision.

However, in the real world, the award of punitive damages has resulted in the following:

- It dramatically changes the value of a case because of the enormous exposure to uncontrollable punitive damages. This in turn facilitates the plaintiff's lawyer extorting a settlement sum from the defendant far in excess of the case's value, simply to avoid being burned by a runaway jury.

- It encourages court or judge shopping. That is, the plaintiff can drift the case into states where the going is easy, as well as lucrative. If you could, you as the plaintiff would haul your defendant into a Mississippi court or certain Illinois courts, where you can usually get the punitive damage issue to a generous jury.
- It completely changes the nature of the lawsuit. The elements of the wrongful conduct are pushed aside for an impassioned pitch directed against the defendant's wealth. This diversion from the purpose of punitive damages is now sanctioned by the *Restatement of Torts*, 3rd edition, section 908.
- It artificially drives up the costs of producing goods and insurance premium costs, simply to facilitate a massive transfer of wealth.

Absent legislative intervention, the only meaningful check lies with our judicial system. The Supreme Court has not imposed caps but has set rough guidelines. It has held outrageous punitive awards are not reasonable, as they are disproportionate to actual damages. A punitive award of over $1 million when the damages consisted of a buyer's hurt feelings over his Mercedes-Benz having been painted the wrong color, in his view, is not just; a redo of the paint job is. The award constitutes an unconstitutional taking from Mercedes-Benz, using the courts.

Since this decision, the court has reversed when the punitive damages bore no relationship to compensatory and has given an upper range of three to five times compensatory as a guideline for lower courts. The court in *Philip Morris v. Williams* put a further restraint on the award of punitive when it reversed an award, where Williams recovered not only for his loss but for that of other smokers similarly situated but not identified as parties to the litigation.

CHAPTER 4

The Health Industry

Tort law and accompanying legislation have severely impacted the health industry. The result is that meaningful health care is no longer economically available to most people, absent the insurance industry or government subsidization. The health industry is one-sixth of our economy; what goes on within that industry affects us all and, therefore, warrants separate treatment. In this chapter, we explore:

- What the health industry was
- What the health industry is
- How doctors are involved
- What role the hospitals play
- People who slip through the cracks

What the Health Industry Was

In the past, the family doctor made periodic visits to the home and was available when needed. One tended to enjoy an intimate relationship with this person. When someone spoke of his or her doctor, it was with a reverence and trust enjoyed by all in the profession. The doctor lived in the community and was known by many in the community. While admittedly doctors lived well, what they were paid was rarely questioned, as they clearly had devoted time and skills to a vitally important aspect of the community's health and well-being.

Equally important is that most doctors don't just take their profession seriously but also work passionately. A physician friend of mine summed it up eloquently: "You know, my most personally rewarding times are spent one-on-one with a patient having a medical problem I might be able to take care of. It is important to me to have that relationship not just with the patient but with the family, which continues, sometimes, generation after generation."

That period is gone, not because doctors today are of a different breed but for the reasons set forth hereinafter.

What the Health Industry Is

How Doctors Are Involved

Physicians say, "All I want to do is treat patients; this is what I was trained to do." Instead, they are confronted with health insurers who are the source of most of their income. This is not of their choosing; doctors are forced into this box by Medicare, the ACA, and other federal legislation that has relentlessly forced the private sector out of the field.

With government intervention comes change in who sets medical standards. These standards doctors must adhere to have been set by people with little or no medical background. As the insurers pick up an ever-increasing percentage of doctors' incomes, they increasingly exert control over how doctors practice their profession.

In addition, doctors are required to fill and file endless forms. They are constantly looking over their shoulders for the government compliance agent or the malpractice attorney. If they want to be paid, there is little they can do to fend off the continuing demands of the government. Doctors—not their assistants—must prepare and file meaningless forms that will never be read. This mindless gesture cuts dramatically into the time they can spend with patients. It puts doctors under needless additional stress.

To shed themselves of malpractice attorneys, doctors must pay relentlessly increasing insurance premiums each year. If they contract with other professionals or hire employees, they must insure them also. For months of each year, they must generate income solely to pay this staggering additional expense of doing business.

Regardless of the care they exercise, they are target defendants when patients seek redress. Even worse, a doctor may well be a defendant in an action initiated by a patient the doctor never treated. Once hooked into litigation, the doctor is pressured by the plaintiff's side, and at times the doctor's own attorney, to come up with money to close a settlement deal. The doctor must weigh the amount demanded against the time that might be spent in consultation with lawyers, as a deposition witness, and in trial. That time is nonrecoverable income lost. It is infuriating for doctors to be forced to arrive at a sum to pay to buy their way out of lawsuits.

When doctors become buried in a lawsuit, they are plunged into a foreign environment. Their vernacular is difficult if not nearly impossible for the jury to comprehend. They must sit and listen to professional witnesses on the other side "snow" the jury, while they find it difficult to communicate with their own lawyers, whose comprehension is sometimes little better than that of a jury.

Today, doctors cannot carry their offices around in a black bag. They must acquire the diagnostic tools to enable them to provide the best care available. They must pay for these extremely expensive tools. If they are forced to borrow money to pay for these tools, they must shoulder the interest expense in addition to paying off the debt.

The first line of precautionary defense is to order tests and other procedures. The ordering doctor seriously questions the need, but when matters sour, it is the test not ordered, the procedure not performed, that provides the basis for the malpractice claim.

In summary, all of those problems contribute to a doctor's frustration, but in addition, the costs must be incorporated into the billing of the client, giving rise to the complaint "Why is medical care so expensive?"

What Role the Hospitals Play

Personal home care is a thing of the past. Both the doctor and the hospital must be more productive to survive. So, today, you go to a doctor's office, or in emergency situations, you are carted off in an ambulance to a hospital at great cost.

If you are having a heart attack, the ambulance brings you to an emergency room where the quality of care is dictated by who is on call, in many cases a general practitioner because a cardiologist is too expensive, and there may not even be one willing to spend evenings at a hospital. Fortunately, this is changing. Cardiologists and other specialists may not be at the emergency room at night but are now able to be called in, resulting in a shorter time before the patient receives the specialized medical treatment needed.

But before you land at an ER, you may be driven all over the area before you find a hospital that can, or will, take you. The reason for your rejection by a hospital is, on the surface, "we are full." However, the decision of whether to accept a patient is influenced by factors such as how the hospital is going to be paid, does the patient have insurance, or is the patient on a federal program so the hospital can be assured of payment. Rejection is motivated by survival, not greed.

While it now seems a national pastime to knock doctors and hospitals, it is also true that hospitals are failing because of the number of admissions who exact expensive care for which they cannot pay. Hospitals therefore exercise discretion in the admission of patients, just to survive. Hospitals oriented to particular communities, operating on the edge, realize they will fail even though they exercise discretion and ultimately sell out to a larger regional firm.

A Higher Level of Care Means More Expensive Care

There are more people in the world; these people are living longer and increasingly have problems, and therefore there is more need for medical care. However, available medical care has outstripped the income to support it. Medical science has dramatically improved medical care. But this improvement comes with a cost—an extraordinary cost.

A new building will cost five times that of the old general hospital. What goes into the building places its total cost out of the reach of local financing. Administrators must go to the bank or find wealthy investors or the new facility will not be built. It is incredibly difficult for a city council to pony up the money for a new facility, knowing it must be reflected in the next tax bill for citizens of the community and ultimately in the political future of that city council.

So, today, new hospitals go up financed. Before the doors open, a monthly interest bill is due the investors or lenders, and this relentless expense goes on, month after month. The CAT scanners, MRI machines, and other expensive diagnostic tools are independently financed and, therefore, are another monthly expense to cover the debt. There now is a need to keep the machine working to generate the income to service this debt. The bottom line is that a hospital must generate a specific amount of money each day the door is open, even before it thinks of paying its labor bill, its electric and water bills, and the other ongoing expenses.

And then enters the insurance company. As soon as a hospital borrows money to build, the lender insists on security that the lender will be paid. When the owner enters into a contract with a general contractor, that owner wants to ensure the work will be done. When the general contractor enters into a contract with a subcontractor or materials supplier, that contractor insists on security of performance. In each of the above cases, an insurance policy and its premium are introduced into the equation of cost. Once the insurance company becomes part of the litigation equation, dramatic changes take place.

The Impact of Insurance

While insurance premiums may well have started at an amount digestible to the insured, that is not the case today. Today, the insurance premium is prohibitively high, to the point where the insured, simply to be able to live with the premium amount, will agree to self-insure up to a point where the reduced premium is within financial reach.

Insurance companies are by contract obliged to provide to the insured a lawyer to defend any claim against the insured, but they reserve the right to select that lawyer. As steady work from an insurance company is highly desired by law firms, an insurance company may end up hiring a lawyer who wins the contract on the golf course or in the local bar. Once securing the continuing contract, the lawyer is inclined to make the real client happy with good results. This frame of mind inevitably pits the lawyer against the insured, who is the client of record. The actual following case, in which I acted as house counsel, illustrates this problem.

The preceding gave some insight into the problems. There are more people living longer. The costs of medical care are increasing to the point where one incident in life can render you insolvent. We solve this dilemma by introducing insurance, purportedly to spread the risk. But we find we have done little more than introduce another layer to the cost of medical care. Solutions have been advanced with varying degrees of merit:

- Curtail malpractice suits by establishing a workable standard of care.
- Award attorney fees and court costs to the prevailing party.

- Introduce legislation that eliminates mindless regulations, retaining only those that directly relate to the quality of health care.

People Who Slip through the Cracks

Notwithstanding the extraordinary costs of medical care coupled with strangling regulatory control, we are plagued with established medical institutions that have lost sight of the very reason for which they exist.

I represented several nursing homes, some owned and some leased by the client. I was asked to intervene when the head administrator of all the facilities felt uncomfortable about the direction a lawsuit was headed. The facts of the case were as follows:

The facilities were confronted with a staggering premium, so self-insured against workers' compensation and general liability coverage up to $400,000, at which point the insurance company must step in and provide coverage.

A worker doing entry-level menial work at a nursing facility decided he preferred a McDonald's hamburger to the lunch provided for the patients and workers at the facility. McDonald's was located at the bottom of a hill. During his noon break, the worker hopped on his motorcycle and took off down the hill to McDonald's. He lost control over the bike and got creamed. His injuries were devastating. He ended up paralyzed from the waist down.

A local hospital gave treatment to the worker at a cost of just under $200,000 and had a lien on any money flowing to the worker from workers' comp.

The worker's lawyer, sensing he could not recover against anybody by filing a personal injury complaint, elected to file a claim under workers' compensation, where the central issue would be whether the worker's act of taking off down the hill for his McDonald's hamburger was within the scope of his employment—a tenuous claim at best but better than a conventional proceeding.

The insurance company, pursuant to its contract obligation, hired its lawyer to represent the facility against the claim. But this lawyer's client of record was not the insurance company; it was the facility. His primary fiduciary duty was owed to the insured.

The administrator of the numerous facilities owed by the insured was confronted by her own attorney, who exerted pressure on her to come up with $400,000—the $200,000 owed to the hospital and $200,000 for the worker and his attorney—"so we can get this matter behind us." A meeting was arranged for the administrator, the attorney hired by the insurance company, and me. The reason I was involved is the administrator no longer trusted her own attorney of record.

The administrator, after being repeatedly pressured by her attorney of record to come up with the full extent of the facility's self-insurance, when there were no facts that would support a claim that the injured worker was in some manner acting within the scope of his employment, exploded and said to the insurance company lawyer, "You make me sick. I pay you more in insurance premiums than I spend for food for my patients, and they eat well."

During this meeting, I settled the issue of whether we were going to come up with $400,000 or any other significant amount and suggested we spend our time preparing for trial. This suggestion was met with reluctance on the part of our attorney, who advised me that these cases all settle. They are never tried. My response was that you never go to trial unprepared, relying on your belief the matter will settle. But the attorney said he didn't need any further preparation. Nevertheless, I prepared for trial.

At the administrator's request, I appeared at trial to ensure the insured's interest was protected. I had settlement authority from the administrator in the event it could be settled. I was also prepared to go to trial.

At the time set for trial, it appeared clear that our attorney, the plaintiff's attorney, and the judge had no intention of trying the case. If it could not settle, it would be continued. Our attorney of record resumed his pitch to have the facility come up with $400,000 to settle the case. I listened to his arguments repeated over and over: "The plaintiff has horrible injuries. He says he will testify he was going down to McDonald's pursuant to a facility policy of letting—actually, encouraging—employees to have their lunches at McDonald's." However, his greatest emphasis was placed on the insured's "obligation" to take care of the worker.

Prior to trial, I ran the following proposal past the administrator: since we all were interested in seeing that the worker was taken care of, we should offer, in full settlement of his claim, to take him into the facility as a patient and take care of him. It certainly would be in his best interest to resolve the matter in that manner. My client initially balked at such an open-ended proposal. But I assured her they would never accept such an offer; they wanted money. She gave me the authority.

When I advised our attorney to make this offer, he balked. The following conversation took place:

"I can't make such an offer. It has to be money."

"Why? If we are here to work out the best solution for the worker, is this not better for him than money, which will be soon gone, and he will be destitute?"

"It just doesn't work that way. The plaintiff's attorney has to be paid. If I make such an offer, it will be rejected by the plaintiff's attorney, and the judge will get mad at me."

"Make the offer. If you won't, I will."

"You can't make the offer—I am the attorney of record."

"If you won't make the offer, I can handle that problem now and take over the suit."

Our attorney reluctantly agreed to make the offer. As expected, it was rejected, and now the motives of all the parties were known. We were not all there to secure the best meaningful benefit for the worker.

Our attorney returned, asking me to come up with some money, any money. I told him, "If we can't settle, then let's go to trial." His response was what I suspected. Nobody was prepared, nor intended, to go to trial, and it would be continued if it was not settled.

I then gave our attorney $75,000 to settle the case. His almost hysterical response was that not only would it be rejected but also he would be chastised by the judge for making it. He nevertheless reluctantly made the offer. It was accepted.

What did the worker get out of the settlement, about $30,000? The rest was split between the unpaid hospital and the worker's attorney.

Our worker was sent down the road with just enough money to buy a new Pontiac with all controls on the steering column. A car he would soon lose. He could not buy gas, let alone maintain the car, as he had no job and was unemployable. The statutory scheme surrounding workers' compensation, for good reason, simply didn't apply to him. Our tort schemes supporting negligence, warranties, and strict liability in tort also excluded him, as he could not point to a tortfeasor.

It is difficult to reconcile our injured worker with the woman who was awarded millions when she dumped a hot cup of McDonalds's coffee on her crotch or the buyer of a new Mercedes-Benz who was awarded an incredible amount because he didn't like the color of his new car, despite the fact that Mercedes-Benz offered to repaint the automobile.

But the point is, this elaborate workers' compensation scheme to provide a safety net for workers has lost the purpose for which it exists.

So, What Can Be Done?

Give the Trial Judge More Discretion
As to the McDonald's and Mercedes-Benz cases, we should give the trial judge much more discretion in disposing of litigation devoid of merit, as opposed to our present system where the judge is on safer ground if the matter goes to the jury and we spin the financial wheel. We should allow the judge more latitude in evaluating whether there is substantial evidence to support a plaintiff's claim—perhaps as much latitude as we give juries in determining the facts of a case.

There is the trial judge's ever-present fear that the court of appeal will search for any evidence as opposed to substantial evidence that might support a plaintiff's claim and reverse the judge's decision. Trial judges do not like to see their names in the advance sheets.

We Need More Flexibility

As to our worker, we should think in terms of providing him with the best future life practical after his self-inflicted injury or other injury falling outside the scope of workers' compensation acts. There is merit to the argument that our courts are ill-suited to handle certain cases. A tribunal outside the field of torts should be empowered to provide training and skills that may make him a productive citizen. If he is unemployable in any capacity, the government should take him under its all-encompassing wing and provide compensable work that he can do, having in mind his limitations.

Accept the Fact Some Cases Require a Professional Trier of Fact

This brings us to a separate suggestion. Certain fields and specializations come into play, and in these cases we cannot expect a lay jury to comprehend the evidence that must be introduced to reach a decision. In the medical field, physicians speak a language incomprehensible to the layperson. So, the parties hire experts—professional experts—to explain the sides of a complex problem. But professional experts in many fields operate in a world all their own. They are called to the witness stand by counsel, they are qualified as experts, and then they are invited to take over the case, answering the ultimate question that should be ascertained by the jury.

But all too often the jury cannot comprehend. They do not know when they are being "snowed" or given the "mushroom treatment." They are reduced to waiting for the ultimate circus performance by counsel, which we caustically refer to as the final argument.

While this is of significance in the health industry, it is applicable in any area where the logic of the situation dictates we are doing a disservice to the adversarial justice system by allowing—no, encouraging—theater in the courtroom.

If we put litigation in the hands of a judge with medical experience, or three judges so talented, and allowed the adversaries to put their best cases forward, we would be far more likely to reach a just result. We would now have the trier of fact on equal ground with the advocates and their experts. We would afford these triers of fact the same deference we presently give juries.

The loser should pay court costs and attorney fees. The loser should pick up all trial costs. Costs may include reasonable attorney fees. The attorney who takes a meritless case would think twice before pursuing the client's claim upon the belief they should be able to squeeze out $20,000 or so for the case's nuisance value. England and other countries allow the winner to be compensated for all costs.

An alternative to having the loser pay all costs would be to allow a party to establish a baseline for disposition. A defendant could offer to settle for judgment in a specified sum. If the plaintiff refused to accept, the plaintiff would be at peril to pick up all costs from that date forward, including reasonable attorney fees, if unable to secure a better judgment than that offered. California has a watered-down version of this remedy. This remedy would give pause to an attorney and client; if they were offered a secure judgment in a specific amount and rejected it, this would establish a new bar the party must exceed.

These measures encourage settlement and are supported by the adage: if both parties are somewhat dissatisfied with the settlement reached, it probably was a good settlement.

We could award interest on the ultimate judgment in tort from the date of the injury. This would apply only to damages that are ascertainable as of the judgment date. We could not allow interest on the speculative continuing damages. Presently, courts are reluctant to do this as the amount cannot be ascertained until judgment time. However, the same courts have no problem in awarding prejudgment interest in other cases such as contract breaches and eminent domain. However, this is a legislative matter, and understandably, legislatures are loath to walk into this quagmire: for example, how do you establish the date interest starts when your damages are accruing up to the date of judgment and sometimes thereafter?

We also need to put a cap on physical pain, mental suffering, or emotional distress. While there is no question such injuries are real, juries are invited to speculate on the amount. Attorneys are invited to put on a show, as it is difficult to present direct evidence either supporting or opposing punitive awards. First, punitive damages should be limited to three to five times compensatory damages. Second, and a far more effective measure, would be to award all punitive damages to the government agency that built the courthouse, supplied the courtroom, and supplied the judge, clerk, and bailiff. See how far that flies with the plaintiffs' bar.

The above solutions are not without criticism. The plaintiffs' trial bar will argue such measures "chill" the filing of complaints, that many meritorious claims would never be filed. The counterargument is that the above suggestions only chill claims of questionable merit. Lawyers, acting in their best interest, will take meritorious cases. Placing a cap on pain and suffering at $250,000 did not dry up claims in states enacting such legislation. It did winnow out those firms that felt they could spend their resources and time on other, more productive litigation.

As stated before, we have a serious ethical problem when the doctor or hospital is compelled to buy liability insurance and assume the first $100,000. First, while we cannot eliminate the ethical problem, we can blunt its impact by allowing the insured to buy liability insurance across state lines. There is no substitute for competition in the marketplace. Second, and more important, we buy insurance because medical costs can be disastrous.

Medical costs are the problem. If they are reduced to a point where most people don't need insurance to survive, we can dramatically change the health care picture for the better.

CHAPTER 5

Administrative Law Courts

In addition to Article III courts—the local superior court, the courts of appeal, and the Supreme Court—there are administrative law tribunals, sometimes referred to as quasi-courts. They are created within legislative acts such as the National Labor Relations Act, our tax court within the Internal Revenue Tax Code, National Traffic and Motor Vehicle Safety Act, and Social Security. State statutes also create these administrative tribunals to dispose of litigation within the scope of their respective acts. These administrative procedures were created in good faith to expediently handle in-house problems.

The problem arises when these quasi-courts become terribly politicized or, worse, corrupted. Let's examine two acts relating to these courts, the National Labor Relations Act and the National Traffic and Motor Vehicle Safety Act.

National Labor Relations Board

The National Labor Relations Act disposes of disputes arising among labor unions, owners, and workers. Under the National Labor Relations Act (NLRA), a board is established to administer the act. This board is the National Labor Relations Board (NLRB). While on the surface the executive branch appoints the members, members are subject to approval by the major labor unions and then confirmed by Congress as a further check before appointment. When Congress refused to confirm NLRB member appointees because of their questionable backgrounds, the Obama administration appointed three unpopular appointees during a period when the president determined Congress was not in session. Fortunately, the Supreme Court reversed this unconstitutional move, holding that Congress, not the president, decides when they are or are not in session.

Administrative law judges try cases arising under the NLRA. Administrative law judges are selected only if labor unions are satisfied they will not cross the hand that feeds them. So, if you are the employer in a dispute with a labor union, plan on having the administrative law judge rule against you. The administrative law judges are not about to lose their job because of a ruling organized labor is unhappy with. But there is more.

A decision by any administrative law judge is given the same deference as a jury determination in a criminal or civil trial. On appeal, any substantive evidence will ensure the decision is affirmed. But it gets worse. An appeal from an administrative law judge is to the NLRB, not a disinterested tribunal. It is only after an appeal of the board's affirming decision that the employer gets the matter before a neutral tribunal, the US Court of Appeals for the Federal Circuit. But by then, there is nothing left to litigate. Any evidence, not the preponderance of evidence, is the measure. So, plan on losing, if you are a third person or employer in an NLRB proceeding against a labor union.

In the interest of continuity of thought, an example I personally experienced is set forth in detail in appendix A. What we learn from appendix A is:

First, if you are dealing with the NLRB's quasi-judicial branch, you must understand that the large labor unions are in control of the process. Administrative law judges and the board are, for all purposes, union certified.

If a dispute arises, the union will quickly file a complaint claiming an unfair labor practice, plunging you into their court system. At the conclusion of a trial before the administrative law judge, the union's counsel will prepare the order for the judge to sign. There is no meaningful consideration of the evidence resulting in an unbiased independent decision based upon the facts of the case.

Second, the decision of the administrative law judge will be affirmed by the board, so there is no meaningful appeal. While you can appeal the board's decision to the circuit court of appeal, their jurisdiction is limited to an inquiry as to whether there is any evidence—not a preponderance of evidence—supporting the decision.

Finally, these tribunals have the power to determine whether a party is guilty of tortious or unlawful conduct. They can take property from one party and give it to another. They can do all this based not upon legislation but, in great part, on regulations drafted by people who are not accountable to the public through the election process.

These regulations have the full force of law because the regulators amassed and ran these regulations through Congress on a Thursday afternoon when the legislators were eager to head home for the weekend. These regulations were made law by legislators who had absolutely no knowledge of what was within these regulations. In fairness, it is pointed out this sad state of affairs occurs in both Democrat and Republican administrations.

National Transportation Safety Board

The National Transportation Safety Board (NTSB) handles disputes that arise within the various forms of transportation, such those that use railroads, highways, water, and air.

This has the same quasi-court structure as the NLRA. You have, at the top, the politically appointed members of the NTSB. You have administrative law judges also politically appointed. There is no physical, ethical, or political separation. All hang out in the same building, on the same floor, in the same wing together with the NTSB administration—a cozy arrangement from which you handle disputes.

You can see the inherent problem that plagues this administrative law system. Our legislators claim they do not have the time to get into the workings of their legislative creations or the regulations that control the legislative and quasi-judicial pr ocesses. The regulators, being entrenched, wrest control of the department from the legislators. When a new legislator arrives on the scene, that person has little background in the very areas they are accountable for, so the easiest path is to just let the regulators continue in control. The regulator then fashions the department to satisfy personal objectives, goals, or political persuasion. The regulator has awesome control over the legislator, as the former can make the latter look good or incompetent, so there is little pushback. There is a strong incentive to go along with the standing program.

While legislators come and go, regulators do not, and they are not accountable to the electorate. It is much easier on the regulators if they set up a structure that doesn't just ease their burden but also gives them absolute control over the very people they are supposed to serve. For example, under NTSB structure, whether a pilot or mechanic obtains or continues to hold the right to fly or maintain an aircraft hinges on the administrator's unbridled determination of whether that person's flying or working on the aircraft constitutes a safety threat. How do you meaningfully test or regulate abuses with such an open-ended measurement?

For example, Bob Hoover, a well-known accomplished pilot who put on air shows, first in a P-51 Mustang, then in a Shrike Commander (a slippery twin-engine aircraft), had his pilot medical certificate revoked. It was not based upon any physical problem. It was based upon some vague reference to an emotional problem, buried in bureaucratic gobbledygook, obviously impossible to pin down.

He ultimately recovered his medical certificate after extensive and expensive litigation. Up to eighty years of age, he continued to fly, put on shows, and entertain people, all without the "emotional problem" that the Federal Aviation Administration (FAA), a department under NTSB, had relied upon. The point of all this is the FAA contended they could take away Bob Hoover's livelihood. Then it was he who had to satisfy them he was not afflicted with an emotional problem. The burden of proof had been improperly reversed.

If you are a pilot having a dispute with the FAA, you are relegated to an administrative law system that is stacked against the pilot. When trial time arrives, the administrative law judge, the administration's counsel who will try the case against the pilot, the regional administrator, and the expert witness they have hired and are relying on to support the administrator's case will all pile into the same plane to be transported to where the trial will be held. They will stay at the same motel, have meals together as a group, and then move on to the next town and the next pilot's trial.

Into this setting the pilot and counsel are plunged. Preparation for trial by the pilot's counsel is all but impossible. If the administrator's counsel elects to not submit to discovery, none will be conducted. In separate instances, I have attempted to conduct discovery related to the factual basis upon which the administrator concluded the pilot was unfit to fly and therefore pulled his medical ticket. In each case, the administrator's counsel refused to make discovery, thereby depriving the pilot of due process. The details of this case, supporting the position taken earlier, are set forth in appendix B.

While the trial may well be conducted properly in decorum and mutual courtesy, the outcome is never in doubt. The expert hired by the administrator will take a look at the pilot's file on the air flight up to the place of trial. Prior to this cursory look-see, the expert will know nothing about the pilot, including physical condition. On cross-examination, the expert will have to admit to having never seen the pilot, never examined the pilot, and never conducted any tests on the pilot, but can argue that isn't really necessary.

Under the system, the substantial evidence rule, medical conclusions are sufficient evidence to carry the issue all the way up through the circuit court of appeal determination.

What is at stake is not just the right to fly; it is the livelihood of many pilots caught in the web. It is their businesses, their lives, on the line. The FAA's callous hypocrisy is difficult to stomach.

In the case where the pilot's medical ticket was pulled, as detailed in appendix B, during the lengthy proceedings to get this ticket back, the FAA found itself in a crack. The pilot whose ticket they had revoked was the only person qualified to give a check ride to another pilot, who needed the positive check ride to earn this multiengine seaplane rating.

The FAA decided they would look the other way, but only for the check ride. In reality, the administrator who was taking the pilot's medical ticket away upon contention the pilot was a threat to the safety of himself and others requested the pilot participate in the check ride.

We must keep in mind the only basis upon which the FAA could take the pilot's ticket was that the pilot was a menace to people. During the check ride, there was no one in the plane who could be pilot in command; the pilot seeking a rating was not qualified to be pilot in command, and the check ride pilot had no medical certificate. This is impermissible per FAA regulations, but under the circumstances, the hypocrisy posed no problem to the FAA. Fortunately, as detailed in appendix B, the pilot eventually did get the medical ticket back, but only after a trial and an unsuccessful appeal by the administrator.

The point of all this is the tortious conduct on the part of those in government who can and do adversely affect the livelihoods of those they are supposed to serve. They walk into the judicial arena with an incredible advantage created by the underlying legislative scheme.

CHAPTER 6

Sovereign Immunity

We find, much to our surprise, that we started off with no right to sue our government for their tortious actions. The same is true with their contractual breaches. This is sovereign immunity. Abraham Lincoln defined "sovereign" as having "no higher authority." Five hundred years ago, in England, the king was the sovereign. He possessed all political power. This included the right of his subjects to bring an action or lawsuit against him if his tortious conduct injured them; he deprived them of this right. It wasn't an accepted doctrine—it was the law, as he was the law. During this period, it was good to be king; it wasn't necessarily good to be his constituents.

Incrementally, the monarchy relinquished this immunity. When the North American colonies took shape, the king of England was still their sovereign. But with the ratification of our Constitution, not only was the king removed as sovereign but government itself stepped aside for a new sovereign.

Our Constitution's preamble says, "We the People, in order to form a more perfect union…do ordain and establish this Constitution." Article 1, Section 1, first sentence, provides, "All legislative powers herein granted are vested in Congress…" Therefore, as to those powers delegated to Congress, the people have relinquished sovereignty. As to all other political powers, they are "reserved to the states or the people"—see the Tenth Amendment to our Constitution.

This is the starting point of our discussion. We find our government, acting though its representatives and employees, from time to time committing tortious acts on its citizens. The question is whether the employees and representatives are accountable or whether the government is responsible as their employer.

Fortunately, the government can waive its immunity and consent to be sued, if it chooses to do so. Federally, it has done so in the Federal Tort Claims Act, as to torts, and the Tucker Act, as to certain contracts. The purpose of these waivers is to make government accountable for its tortious conduct, just as citizens are responsible for their wrongful acts.

However, citizens who seek redress from tortious acts of the government must bring themselves within the scope of these acts before acquiring standing in court. Citizens must satisfy the federal court that the matter presents a federal question, that there is diversity, or that other specific requirements are met before that court can exercise jurisdiction. Jurisdiction is a condition precedent to the court exercising judicial power.

State constitutions and legislative acts fall into line with federal law providing limited waiver of immunity, so the same problems arise when states, counties, cities, and districts commit tortious acts. You, as an injured citizen, must prove you fall within this waiver or consent to be sued before pursuing a lawsuit against a public entity, federal or state.

But this limited immunity, coupled with limited waiver, coupled with administrative law, reaches deeply into the fundamental premise upon which we self-govern. Repeatedly in history, where government is the wrongdoer, we have examples where there is a wrong but no meaningful remedy. As an example, at the outset of the Civil War, there was a publisher named Merryman who wrote abrasive articles attacking President Lincoln; he was thrown into a federal stockade. While the US Supreme Court, under Presiding Chief Justice Roger Taney, could issue an order to show cause why Merryman should either be tried or released, then serve the order on the stockade commander and the president, the judicial order could be, and was, ignored by the president. The presiding justice was helpless to do anything further. In short, a judicial decree is of no force or effect unless the other two branches of government voluntarily submit to and carry out the judicial decision.

As a further example, President Franklin Roosevelt in January 1942 issued an executive order uprooting and interning 118,000 Japanese American citizens for the period of the war. In doing so, he opened up a due process constitutional issue. There was no evidence of disloyalty, no hearing, no due process afforded these American citizens. As the war dragged on, it became increasingly evident these Japanese American citizens were no threat. They in fact gathered up their youth and delivered them to the US Army, and they would serve as the 442nd, the most decorated unit in World War II.

Notwithstanding, when the legal challenge to this executive order reached the Supreme Court in *Korematsu v. U.S.*, our Supreme Court fell into political line, concluding the president's act was within his powers as commander in chief. Swept aside were the constitutional restraints on that power. In 1945, when the war was all but over, the Supreme Court partially reversed itself in *Endo v. U.S.*—the United States Supreme Court concluded that Endo could leave the internment compound for limited periods of time. However, at this point, the government's position had deteriorated to the point of nonexistence; Japan was not a threat, and Japanese Americans had established their undivided loyalty to their country, the United States of America.

But clearly their internment was wrongful conduct. The government's persisting in holding the citizens in concentration camps was wrong each day of internment. However, no effort was made to right these wrongs. There was no appropriate remedy.

After WWII and before the Korean conflict, President Truman, as part of federal intervention in a labor dispute, seized the steel industry factories. The argument advanced by Solicitor General Holmes Baldridge to Judge David Paine justifying the action is frightening. Baldridge advanced the position that Truman had absolute power to seize the factories, and the judiciary was helpless to interfere with the decision and action.

This argument goes to the heart of our founding principles of separation of powers, balance of powers, and checks and balances. Fortunately, Truman went down in judicial flames over this tortious act of the executive branch of government taking over private property.

Finally, our Affordable Care Act (ACA), aside from the questionable tactics employed to secure congressional passage, has been unilaterally changed from time to time by executive order, not by congressional act, in violation of the separation of powers doctrine. The administration, not Congress, has changed timelines and deferred implementation of provisions within the act when it was politically expedient to do so.

Government forcing people to buy insurance from a private corporation is wrong. Government taking from one class and giving to another by subsidizing insurance premiums is tortious conduct. In each case, the Supreme Court held that the government did not have the power to do what it did, if we limit our inquiry into the enumerated powers found in the second paragraph of Article I, Section 8.

It does not correct the wrongs by holding that the government had the power to do so as a tax under the first paragraph of Section 8 of Article I. Thus far, this conduct is immune from correction by the judicial branch of the federal government. If correction is to come, it will be from the legislative branch of government.

In this discussion, we will not dwell on the direct, easy-to-answer questions, such as liability when a government employee driving a government car on government business slams into a citizen. The Federal Tort Claims Act provides both jurisdiction and a remedy. Instead, let's delve into the shadowy areas where an uneven playing field is the norm and injury has taken place, but there appears to be no remedy.

As examples illustrating the point, in my experience representing landowners, I have run into the following walls erected by government under its immunity protection, coupled with erecting an uneven playing field when the citizen seeks redress.

Assessment without Benefit

To understand this problem, consider the following example. A public entity wants to impress a special assessment on your real property for a proposed public project that will be of no value, no benefit (general or special) to your property. They do so because your property increases their tax base for imposing assessments. The statute under which they proceed requires a special benefit to your property as a condition precedent to their power to impress a special assessment against it.

At the legislatively required public hearing, the landowner and owner of the business in question make a presentation demonstrating graphically and through witnesses that in no manner could the completed project be of any benefit, let alone special benefit, to the property. The government calls one "expert" witness. He is the financial expert who sold the project to the city council, who drafted the necessary documents, and who will be financially rewarded if the project goes though.

He is asked one question: "In your opinion, will all the properties in question be specially benefited?" With his yes, the ballgame is over as far as our courts are concerned. His yes is sufficient evidence to support the city council's predetermined action. The judicial measure is not a preponderance of evidence or even consideration of the landowner's evidence. So much for due process. There is no remedy in tort or injunction to prevent the taking of money from the landowner in exchange for an illusory special benefit.

We have both legislatively and judicially delegated to the local city council, board of directors, and board of supervisors the trial function of settling disputes. Their fact-finding power is given the same deference we give juries. As demonstrated, we have given to the public entity who wants to assess the property, whether benefited or not, the function of an unbiased jury. We, as well as they, know what they intend to do. They have before them the already voluminous documents they must sign at the end of the public hearing. After the close of the public hearing, they call for the question and then approve and sign the assess-ment documents creating the special district.

When the landowner/loser before the local legislative body appeals from the local decision to our courts, they do not give the plaintiff a trial de novo—that is, a new trial—but require the plaintiff to demonstrate from the record that error has occurred. The financial consultant's yes closes the judicial door. This fraudulent proceeding strikes at the heart of due process.

Taking without Compensation

In a similar proceeding, an irrigation district wanted to increase an existing water canal capacity by increasing the height of the berm. In doing so, it had to deal with a new angle of repose for the outside slope that would extend another twenty to thirty feet into the adjacent farmers' fields. Therefore, the district had to condemn these narrow strips to provide for the toe of the outside berms. Because of the unusual shape of the condemned property, twenty feet by four hundred feet, its fair market value was severely limited, but not enough to hire a lawyer and take the matter to trial. Notwithstanding, both an easement and fee simple have value. Both our federal Constitution and state constitutions require a public entity to pay just compensation when they take private property.

The board held its public hearing and adopted the Need and Necessity Resolution (we need the property, and it is necessary to a public project), giving the district the authority to condemn these adjacent panels in fee simple. It then gave its right-of-way agents instructions to approach the landowners with a deal they could not refuse. In essence, it was: We can condemn in fee simple if we want, but we only need an easement over the twenty-foot strip of your land. If you will gift deed an easement, we will go away, and you can use the twenty-foot strip as best you can. Refuse to give us the easement, and we will condemn in fee simple, and you will lose all use of the strip.

Out of about 120 landowners, all but 7 caved in and gave the easements without compensation. As to the 7 holdouts, the district filed its complaint in condemnation to take the fee simple. The attorneys for the landowners argued the district did not need the fee simple—it needed only the easement—and presented evidence from the district's right-of-way agents confirming the landowners' assertion and the modus operandi of the district to coerce landowners to gift deed the easements. The trial judge held for the district, concluding proof of fraud was not relevant to the district's legislative power to condemn in fee simple or for an easement.

The Supreme Court of California had already ruled that with the enactment of the Need and Necessity Resolution, all issues, save the fair market value, were decided legislatively and nonjusticiable. The sense I had was that the district court of appeal would have given relief but was bound by the supreme court decision, so understandably sided with the condemnor. A petition to the Supreme Court of California was denied, and our judicial sun had set.

Our courts are reluctant to decide cases on the merits where their decision may infringe upon legislative power delegated to the legislative body. They will not delve into the legislative body's ulterior motives. They will look aside when fraud is evident. This frame of mind is not restricted to local matters. The two ACA (Affordable Care Act) cases evidence a reluctance, more accurately, an irritation, when the legislative loser plunges the matter into the judicial arena.

Taking for a Private Purpose

Kelo v. New London (2005) 545 U.S. 469 is a case where six landowners of beautifully located homes on the banks of the Thames River in New London, Connecticut, had their homes condemned and removed by a city's agency so the properties could be turned over to Pfizer Inc. to be used as a parking lot for its soon-to-be-built home office. The issue was whether parking lot use by a private corporation was a public use as required by our Fifth and Fourteenth Amendments. Our Supreme Court held that this acquisition and transfer to a redevelopment agency was within the condemning powers of the city. As an afternote, Pfizer changed its mind, the developer could not get the financing, and the Kelo lot remains vacant.

The preceding examples illustrate the helplessness associated with bad faith exercised by government agencies, for which there is no remedy. Courts are reluctant to get involved as the specter of immunity and legislative acts, as opposed to a justiciable issue, are thrust forth as a defense. Sadly, I have been told by judges more than once, "Your remedy is at the voting booth, not here."

CHAPTER 7

Summary

In this field of tort law, we have problems, some solvable and some not. Some have little expectancy of resolution because under our Constitution, we delegate power to Congress to govern us. As most of any proposed change must come from Congress, absent its cooperation, little can be done by the individual.

There is a striking difference between the legislator of the early 1800s in the exercise of intelligent good faith and those in Washington today. There is striking difference between the common person on the street of the 1800s and those today. For this reason, we should take a look at the people and legislators of that era. They must have gotten something right, or we would not have prospered as we did.

Alexis de Tocqueville left France and traveled to and stayed in the newly formed United States for well over a decade. He traveled throughout the States, reducing his observations to voluminous notes. These observations were reduced to a four-volume work, *Democracy in America*.

Tocqueville was both accurate and credible. He had no social or political ax to grind. He is cited as authority today by politicians, historians, lawyers, and judges. This occurs when the issue at hand requires delving into what was taking place in early 1800s. I make no attempt to relate all his observations, only those I feel reflect on our political, economic, and cultural atmosphere today.

Tocqueville came from a country where the people on the street played little or no active role in the politics and governance that controlled them. They were content to let others shoulder the burden. It was only when governance became unbearable did people rise up, participate in a revolution, and then fall back to their inactive role.

In America he was astonished to find a people who took an active role in their governance. People selected their town leaders. These leaders established periodic public meetings in the town square where the problems, both local and national, were thrashed out.

People felt they had a role—no, a duty—to participate in self-governance. They felt they were part and parcel of their community and willingly discharged—no, relished in discharging—that obligation. They attended these meetings, had their say, and for the most part accepted the majority consensus. There was an internal cohesiveness.

People did not run for office. They did not have exhaustive fund-raisers just to get jobs in Washington. Washington was not a desirable place to live. The streets were rutted dirt and mud; you had to hop and skip down the road to avoid the raw sewage flowing down the ruts. People wore perfume to cover up the body odor that comes when you take a bath once a month or so.

The selection of House and Senate members was made in the city square by the elders with active participation by the people. A man was selected to go to Washington because he was good at what he was doing in the community. He was a local success story. He went to Washington reluctantly, solely because he felt he had a duty to serve his time in Washington. It was an obligation he owed to his community. He relished the end of his term so he could return to his business or profession and resume his life.

Legislative Character—Alexander Hamilton

Legislators differed dramatically from those we have today. Alexander Hamilton is a good example. Hamilton had a comfortable life in the affluent—no, elitist—section of New York. He was selected by Governor Clinton to be the third delegate to the 1877 Philadelphia Convention. The other two were little more than the governor's lackeys. Hamilton agreed to go to Philadelphia because he believed something good would happen there, and he wanted to participate.

During the early stage of the convention, two events occurred that soured Hamilton. First, he advanced to the delegates his choice of structure of the new government closely paralleling the British Parliament. The other competing proposal was that of James Madison, establishing a three-branch government. The delegates unceremoniously rejected Hamilton's effort to pattern a new American government after anything British. Hamilton swallowed his pride and remained an active participant in the convention.

The second event was his single vote on each issue was buried by the other two delegates who voted in opposition at every turn. The merits of his position were of no consequence. It soon appeared clear to Hamilton he was accomplishing nothing by attending the convention, and he could use his time more effectively in New York, so he left the convention, leaving the two Clinton associates as sole representatives of New York.

Later, the two remaining delegates from New York left in a huff when their positions were not embraced by the other delegates. This left Madison and Washington with no delegates from New York. Without New York in the fold, the convention would fail. New York's size, economic impact, and geographical position made it indispensable.

Madison contacted Hamilton and requested—no, begged—that Hamilton agree to return. Hamilton again swallowed his pride and returned to Philadelphia and actively participated in working out the multitude of problems that had to be resolved in order for the three-branch government to fly. When time came to vote on the final draft of our Constitution, when Hamilton attempted to cast his vote on behalf of New York, he was stopped by a delegate who raised a point of order; namely a state had to have at least two delegates present to vote. This added humiliation was somewhat blunted when Washington intercepted any repeat of the procedural block rule and expressly asked Hamilton to sign the Constitution.

But it does not stop there. When Hamilton returned to New York to sell this new Constitution and obtain New York's ratification, he found opposition already in full force. Well-written essays were being circulated attacking the Constitution. Hamilton met this opposition by publishing essays supporting the Constitution. He enlisted the help of John Jay and James Madison, who, in total, ground out eighty-five essays that swung the vote for ratification. Today, we refer to this effort as the Federalist Papers. The essays were in opposition to the Anti-Federalist Papers. Today, these essays are referred to, and used as authority, by lawyers, judges, and legislators.

What is the significance of this segment of this book? Hamilton put aside his preferred form of government. He suffered repeated humiliation, yet he persisted and as a result made significant contributions to the Constitution we have today. He then initiated and carried out production of one of the most significant political documents, the

Federalist Papers. These eighty-five essays secured New York's ratification of our Constitution and continue to serve us well, 220 years later. Why did he do it? The answer will seem quaint to some readers, but it shouldn't. Hamilton placed his love for his country ahead of his self-interest.

Today's Legislator

Today, we have little active participation by the average person in his or her governance. Many people do not even know who their representatives, senators, or vice president are. But far worse, when their ignorance surfaces, they snicker. There is no feeling on the part of the electorate that they owe to their community the duty to actively know what is going on, let alone participate. Our participation is reduced to complaining when legislators do what we disagree with or fail to do what they promised to do.

Today, our prospective candidates for office extol the virtue of credentials that come with legislative experience, a laughable argument in the 1800s; they are lauded and praised when they raise enormous amounts of other people's money to finance their campaigns. George Washington's presidential campaign consisted of inviting some of his friends over on a Sunday afternoon, and everybody got drunk.

How does the preceding information fit into tort reform? We have delegated to legislators the power we once had to bring about tort change. Many of the problems enumerated herein can only be rectified by the legislature. However, in many cases, we have the problem because of our legislators.

In my view, the legislator today would not be qualified to carry the briefcase of Hamilton, Washington, Madison, Adams, or Jefferson. If we adopt President Kennedy's assessment, they also lack cognitive skills and wisdom; when addressing guests at a White House exclusive dinner, President Kennedy noted: "Never has there been in this room such an assembly of knowledge, wisdom and experience, other than when Jefferson dined alone."

The legislator today simply lacks character and has questionable wisdom. Therefore, the likelihood of the legislator today acknowledging his past failures and changing legislation is not good.

So, what can we, as individuals, do?

As individuals, we have little impact. But as organized groups, we can influence our legislators. You get a legislator's attention when you serve a petition signed by 10 percent of the constituents, followed up by an intelligent, meaningful presentation of the constituents' expressed concerns supported by facts.

When the legislator is convinced this group's numbers will swell and not go away, and that they will unseat the legislator at the first opportunity, that official will find it in his or her best interest to do what was promised during the last campaign.

That said, when consumers of legal services are confronted with controversy or, worse, litigation, they are inundated with negative surprises. Understandably, when embroiled, sometimes involuntarily, in litigation, they experience problems as set forth in the body of this book. The following suggestions are submitted for addressing these barriers and quagmires.

The Timeline Sinkhole

As discussed before, this is a problem with both lawyers and judges. The lawyer can reduce the time period by taking the following steps:

- File the complaint in a timely manner.
- Insist defendants file their responses promptly.
- File your notice to set the matter for trial soon after the matter is at issue. You can regulate pretrial discovery when you know when the matter will be tried as of a specific date.
- Get your pretrial discovery over. Don't let it drag out. When you have essentially completed discovery, both sides should have a good idea where the lawsuit is going. At this point, all counsel should attempt to settle the case. If necessary, they can employ the services of the judge who can lend substance, a euphemism for pressure, to the settlement

proceedings. Your interest in settling does not suggest weakness; it evidences common sense.

- Make an accurate assessment of the time needed for trial. If it is a two-day trial, clearly state the matter will take two days and see if counsel are willing to fit into a Thursday and Friday trial date in the event another matter settles or concludes trial on Wednesday. This accomplishes multiple good things. You get the matter to trial much earlier. You keep the courtroom and judge functioning throughout the week. You shorten the trial calendar.

- Explore other venues to dispose of the dispute that all parties trust, such as arbitration or referral to a seasoned lawyer.

- Avoid continuances like the plague. It upsets the trial calendar. The judge will have to squeeze you in at some later date, thereby disrupting the court's trial calendar and requiring other parties in other suits to adjust. Those parties, who are prepared to go to trial, must now go through trial preparation again as a precautionary measure, at their expense. Unless the judge can fit another case into the slot, the courtroom is dark.

- Finally, communicate with the client. When you can't move the case along any faster, inform the client of your problems. If you are reluctant to explain why, the problem may well be with you.

The High Cost

A delicate balancing act is assumed by the lawyer when taking a case. The more depositions, the more interrogatories, and the more motions to produce, the more income to the lawyer. However, the lawyer is not hired to advance personal financial interests; the lawyer is there for the client's best interests. Therefore, the lawyer should refrain from duplicative investigation. In fact, the lawyer must measure the value to the client when engaging in any expensive discovery activity.

The malpractice counsel is constantly looking over the attorney's shoulder. After a case is lost, there is little compassion for the attorney's excuse, "I didn't think it was necessary," when that which was not done proves to be not just necessary but critical to the client's case.

We need to clear roadblocks to early settlement of suits. There is no reason why the attorneys for the parties, after acquainting themselves with core issues and conducting sufficient discovery to confirm the probative facts that will control the outcome, should not initiate and complete settlement of the dispute. If both sides, after agreeing to a settlement, are somewhat uncomfortable about the agreement, thinking, "I wonder how much I left on the table?" it was probably a good settlement.

Finally, you, as the lawyer, must communicate with the client. Openly discuss the balancing act you must resolve. Get the client involved in these financial and tactical matters; listen and then inform the client what you intend to do. It is your call, but the client is entitled to input. Remember, in the back of a client's mind is that question of the attorney's loyalty. Loyalty is something that is earned. Loyalty is something easily lost.

Joint Liability

Joint liability creates two conflicting principles. The first is to ensure through our court system that the plaintiff is made whole. In joint liability jurisdictions, we make all defendants liable for all damages. This goes a long way toward accomplishing that goal. In these jurisdictions, the plaintiff's counsel can be heard to say: "All I need to do is find one deep pocket and stick him with 1 percent liability, and I will be paid in full."

However, joint liability has its negative side. To the extent you take property from a defendant beyond the percentage of fault, you are taking the defendant's property and giving it to a plaintiff without a legitimate basis for this transfer of wealth.

In several-liability jurisdictions, we recognize that multiple defendants are not always equally responsible for plaintiffs' injuries. So, we allow plaintiffs to get their judgment in the full amount and then sit back and let the defendants in a later hearing sort out among themselves what percentages of liability are assignable to each defendant. When these percentages are reached, the defendants are liable only for their own percentage of the total judgment amount.

As a compromise, the *Restatement of Torts*, 3rd edition, argues we should adopt that procedure, but if any responsible defendant is not able to respond to his or her portion of the obligation, others must step in and assume this additional load. In practical impact, we are back to making the plaintiff whole at any cost. The compromise is that all defendants share in the additional load, as opposed to dumping everything on the shoulders of a single deep-pocket defendant.

My preference would be several liability, for several reasons. Joint and several liability encourages the plaintiff's counsel to forage for a deep-pockets defendant, even though that defendant may at best be marginally responsible. Once that deep-pockets defendant is roped in, the plaintiff concentrates energy on sticking Deep Pockets with some percentage of the liability—1 percent is sufficient. There should be no overriding principle that ensures every plaintiff full recovery in all situations. Unfortunately, some plaintiffs pick the wrong defendants.

The Collateral Source Rule

My position is that we should stop prohibiting relevant evidence on the issue of damages, which enables plaintiffs to recover more than their total loss. It is argued that we should keep the rule, because the alternative allows the defendant to escape the full extent of the damage recovery. But for the collateral source rule, the defendant gets the windfall, not the plaintiff. There is merit in both conflicting arguments.

You can look on this argument from a different perspective. Windfall connotes partially escaping punishment for your wrong. We punish defendants for their acts, in addition to first making plaintiffs whole. Of course, plaintiffs do have an additional remedy—the right to seek recovery of punitive damages, thereby punishing the defendants and financially rewarding the plaintiffs themselves.

Punitive damages, as opposed to application of the collateral source rule, at least meets the issue directly, but comes with the problems resulting from handling the problem by indirection and is plagued with the problems treated in the section on punitive damages.

Coupled with the above argument is the contention that regardless of whether we have a contingent fee agreement or payment at an hourly rate, the plaintiff never receives the full amount of the judgment. That application of the collateral source rule allows the injured plaintiff to recover at least a part of the loss. This self-serving argument is hardly laudable when advanced by the very person who reduces the injured plaintiff's award by recovery of the attorney's fees. Properly viewed, this is a backdoor attempt to recover attorney fees when by statute none are recoverable.

Attorneys who are genuinely obsessed with making the client whole could reduce their own attorney fees, or perhaps, overcome with a fit of altruism, waive them. We all know that is not going to fly.

Contingent Fee Agreement

There is laudable support for the contingent fee agreement. Some clients with legitimate causes of actions would not be able to get into court absent a contingent fee agreement. It is the attorney who risks time and resources with no assurance he or she will recover these expenses. It is the risk/reward equation that gives rise to the problems, not when the case is lost and nobody gets anything, but when success gives rise to extraordinary attorney fees.

It has been argued the court should step in and restructure the fee agreement to reflect actual time spent, complexity of the issues, and the risk/reward equation. But doing so would seem an unwarranted intrusion into the private contractual relationship between attorney and client. What is worse—it's after the fact. There is potential for when we allow others to decide who wins and who loses.

We should keep in mind that when the client comes into the lawyer's office, the lawyer engages in the initial screening. The attorney ferrets out the clearly meritless cases from those that have all three of the elements necessary to a suit with merit; first, there must be a defendant who can respond; second, it must have been the defendant's act that caused injury to the plaintiff; and finally, there must be significant injury or damages.

The resolution of these disputes, if unresolvable between the attorney and the client, should be handled expeditiously by a judge or independent third party with an adequate background to make a knowledgeable decision.

Product Liability

With strict liability in tort, we have simply gone too far. To sue a seller, there is no requirement that the product be defective or that this defect caused the injury; the seller simply has to put it on the market and any reasonable use of the product results in liability. Soon lost is the fundamental purpose for imposing strict liability in tort—that is, providing consumer protection for that narrow class of goods that pose an extraordinary risk of injury. This flies in the face of the premise that one who unjustly injures others should respond.

Instead, liability is determined upon the inquiry about who should shoulder this risk of loss. We then proceed from the premise that every plaintiff should not leave our courts empty-handed, when the defendant can always buy insurance coverage and we cannot expect all potential plaintiffs to secure insurance coverage.

What is the ultimate result? The cost of tort litigation goes up. Insurance premiums double and then double again, not because of the one in a hundred that results in a staggering judgment. Ninety percent of all suits settle. But they settle for an amount that takes into consideration the possibility that the one in a hundred may come along. With each increase, those who seek insurance cannot afford it so accept self-insurance as the only out. This is the cost we as consumers pay—not the insurance companies, not the lawyers. This is a cost not just to those who pay for insurance premiums. It is reflected in an increase in the cost of goods to the consumer.

Client Concerns about Attorney's Interests

Often the attorney is placed in an ethical conundrum. Loyalty to the client is not some shade of gray; it is either black or white. You are either loyal completely or not loyal at all. Loyalty does not hinge on whether it serves your best interest to be so.

The attorney wants the insurance company's business. It constitutes a significant percentage of the lawyer's total income; nevertheless, the attorney represents the insured, not the insurance company. Fiduciary duty is owed to the client. Conduct must be consistent with that obligation. The client is entitled to something more than lukewarm loyalty. The attorney must be something greater and beyond.

This unrelenting duty at times may well conflict with what the attorney considers good trial tactics. Intelligent cordial discussions between opposing counsel cannot be poisoned by a showing of obnoxious belligerence. At times I have found it beneficial to my clients' interests to have lunch with opposing counsel, laying the foundation for mutual respect and, from there, settlement.

The bottom line is that counsel must strike a balance between being courteous and respectful and appearing to be too cozy with opposing counsel. Again, as in previous problems, candid discussion between client and counsel can allay any fears or apprehension on the part of the client. Communication engenders trust.

Bureaucracy Overtaking Democracy

The core problem with our administrative law system is that we have worked ourselves into a bureaucratic hole. Our legislators have shifted their responsibilities to place law onto the shoulders of the unelected, people who are not accountable to the electorate. While the people from time to time may refresh the elected heads, the bureaucrats remain entrenched year after year, unaffected by what they have done or done poorly.

Our founders worked hard to establish checks and balances, but there was no need for an effective check on the power acquired by the bureaucrat. Not so today. With present-day administrative law, inherent conflicts go to the very core of good government. The electorate elects their representatives, who are duty bound to represent the interests of the electorate. But that is not the way it is, or was. Nicholas II, the last emperor of Russia, complained, "I do not rule Russia; ten thousand clerks do."

A member of the House of Representatives is running for office at all times. It becomes a primary goal, and for some, the only goal. Staff is selected for reasons other than competency to accomplish the purpose and promises made to get elected. It is far more important for staff to assist the representative in getting reelected, so these skills become all important. The same mind-set controls executive appointments. For the most part, appointments are made on the basis of what the applicant accomplished for the executive during the prior election.

But there is a big difference between two classes of bureaucrats. One class is people selected by the elected officials who sink or swim with their appointers. However, the other class consists of established bureaucrats immune from losing their jobs along with their bosses. They are not directly accountable to the electorate. They are protected by complex regulations framed to provide isolation from accountability, coupled to job security. They are all but impossible to dislodge, and they know it.

Some are content to live out their working careers without rocking the boat. But some are eager to expand their power over the people they are duty bound to serve. They do so by creating regulations that accomplish that goal; then they administer these regulations to suit their goals and preserve their job security. The establishment bureaucrats create regulations that become law, then more regulations that are designed to destroy an even playing field between themselves and the very people they are obligated to serve; disputes arise between those who are to be served and those who serve.

Regulations are designed to make the regulator's job easier and the life of the person who is supposed to be served immeasurably more difficult. In a labor dispute, the union can simply claim an unfair labor practice—unfair to whom?

If a pilot goes before the NTSB, the administrators can simply claim they feel that the pilot, if allowed to fly, will compromise safety. What kind of measurable standard is that? How does one check abuses with that as the measure of power? But far worse, the administrators can reach this nebulous conclusion and pursue the matter to trial, without knowing the pilot, examining the pilot, or becoming acquainted with other probative facts related to the case.

Whether the department is the NLRB, the NTSB, Social Security, or the IRS, the administrative law judge decides the case. That determination is then submitted to the board as an appeal from the decision. Only after the board has rubber-stamped the administrative law judge's decision can the employer, or the pilot, or the Social Security recipient, or the taxpayer lodge an appeal to an independent tribunal. However, by that time, there is little left to litigate. *Any substantial evidence will support the administrative law judge's decision.*

It is argued that as to the IRS, the taxpayer has an alternative. That person can pay the tax, then file a complaint in the federal district court. For some well-heeled taxpayers, this is a meaningful alternative and is, in fact, exercised from time to time. But for some others, if not most, the alternative is illusory. Either you can't pay the tax in the first place, or if you can, you do not have the additional resources to hire the lawyer and proceed through the Article III court system.

Far more insidious, with accumulated power, the regulator has something to sell. Enter the special interest with some form of difficult-to-trace quid pro quo for the regulator's "cooperation." The regulator stands aside and lets the lobbyists create the legislation or assists the lobbyists in doing so. The lobbyists understandably advance their interests, not the public's interest. James Madison, in *Federalist 10*, eloquently described the problem as the almost-impossible-to-control "faction."

Next is the regulator who purchases for the government and sells for the government. This is an awesome power but also an invitation to abuse and corruption. It is the regulator who agrees to pay absurd amounts for purchased property. It is the regulator who controls the sale of government property. This activity of government smells of corruption—corruption that never results in discipline to the individual committing the tortious acts.

I represented a gyro repair facility and was personally exposed to an incident that demonstrates the nature of the problem. As it is voluminous, it has been attached as appendix C. But the following paragraphs are the takeaways from this event.

The taxpayer pays over $50,000 per remanufactured gyro because the government purchasing agent has developed a working arrangement with certain sellers, who in turn have working arrangements with other buyers and sellers. When we get to the end of the chain, that is, the gyro facility, who is actually is going to fill the order for $6,000 per gyro, the producer must go back up through the chain—his immediate buyer, and from there through each intermediary who knocks down a profit ranging up to doubling the price while contributing nothing to the transaction—until the government purchasing agent agrees to pay over $50,000 for each gyro to the seller with whom he has an arrangement.

When somebody blows the whistle and finally asks, "Why are we paying over $50,000 each for these gyros?" everybody scurries for cover, protecting themselves and the purchasing agent from being accountable for this hideous disservice to the taxpayer.

Enter the legal department, who is given marching

orders to recover the absurd purchase price from anybody who is in the purchase and sale chain. The legal department has a serious problem. There is nothing wrong with the re-manufactured gyros; they work and were in service. Hence the nameplate issue surfaces to emasculate the wrongdoing of the purchasing agent.

There is nothing new here. James Madison in *Federalist 10* lamented the growth of the "faction" in the pursuit of achieving its goal corrupts government. He pragmatically accepted the fact we cannot eliminate the faction with-out offending the freedoms found in our Constitution. However, he somewhat wistfully hoped that competing factions would blunt the damage done by any particular faction. Today, such hope is misplaced. There is no effective check on the regulator or his boss, who is in bed with the lobbyists. Once the lobbyists own the legislator or regulator or both, the remedy is to cover up the corruption.

The acts of deceit and concealment as detailed in ap-pendix C must be viewed in the following context. This is tortious conduct, a wrong for which there is no meaningful "appropriate" remedy. This is not just a dispute between private parties pursuing their respective interests. This is government pursuing the very people it is obliged to serve. We give government a leg up when it is involved in liti-gation. We give it limited immunity. We give it a level of freedom from accountability for its actions. We give it un-limited resources to circle the wagons and pursue litigation.

In our matter, by statute, the government gives itself the power to seal a court file so nobody, including defendants, can even ascertain they are defendants or the nature of the charges until the government decides to say something. None of these privileges are afforded the private litigant. We should keep in mind a complaint, as filed, is a public record.

With these tactical and substantive advantages must come an obligation to pursue the government's interests on at least the ethical level we demand of the private party embroiled in litigation. However, in my opinion, the rectitude demanded of government must be much higher. How can the citizen respect government absent such an obligation? When the sovereign does wrong, it is no less a tort than when the citizen is the tortfeasor.

This is not just me ranting. Justice Oliver Wendell Holmes eloquently stated: "Men must turn square corners when dealing with the government."[1] John MacArthur Maguire and Philip Zimet of Harvard Law School developed this principle further, adding, "It is hard to see why government should not be held to a like standard of rectangular rectitude when dealing with its citizens."[2]

---

1. *Rock Island, Arkansas & Louisiana Railroad Company v. United States*

2. John MacArthur Maguire and Philip Zimet, "Hobson's Choice and Similar Practices in Federal Taxation," *Harvard Law Review 8*, no. 8 (1935): 1281; Justice Carter solidified this concept into law in *Farrell v. County of Placer*.

Misusing the vast powers of government to extort money from the gyro shop falls far short of the ethical standard Justice Holmes and Maguire and Zimet had in mind. Employing the shabby trial tactics of concealment and deceit is particularly reprehensible when perpetrated by government. It cannot be overly stressed; the government is the agent owing a fiduciary duty to those it serves. In any courtroom, government has a commanding hand; the party directly causing or bringing about the litigation gets a free ride. That party's attorney fees and costs are paid for by the taxpayer.

I would like to suggest the following remedial measures.

First: the legislator must be conversant with the laws passed and the regulation being converted into law. If these are too voluminous and complex, the problem is with the regulation. Relevancy and succinctness are achievable virtues. There must be some check on the legislators to ensure they know what they are sanctioning. Making them accountable other than at the ballot box for the tragic results of application of the law would be a good start.

Second: regulations should be periodically reviewed, meaningfully reviewed by an independent third party, not the very people who wrote the regulation. This independent party must submit an intelligible, comprehensive written report, concluding the regulations should be dropped or modified or the reasons why they should be retained.

To argue that we already have checks and balances on these regulations and that is an admission of whatever you have done in the past has not been meaningful or credible. It has not worked. Instead, the order of the day is to have the agency investigate itself. Again, this is an issue for our legislative branch to solve with meaningful legislation that provides for transparency and reform.

Finally: require government to adhere to the same ethical standards it impresses on its citizens. In our three-branch government, we separate powers. We take pride in this separation, as it is a meaningful check on the accumulation of power by any particular faction. However, there is a drawback to adherence to this division of power, as we have seen repeatedly at Senate or House committee hearings, where the legislative branch attempts to exercise its legislative oversight.

However, it is repeatedly stonewalled by the bureaucrat witness, who is smugly secure in the knowledge that while Congress can expose wrongdoing on the part of the bureaucrat, Congress must refer its discovery of criminal or ethical misconduct to the executive department for prosecution. But sadly, it is helpless to compel the US attorney to prosecute, resulting in no corrective measure being taken.

However, Congress is not without remedies. First, it can cut off funding to corrupt agencies. Second, it can impeach and remove bureaucrats. Both are meaningful remedies. However, again, sadly, Congress elects to publicly beat its chest over the wrongful conduct and enacts neither remedy. Therefore, the bottom line is: we have tortious conduct, but the government entity, acting in its own best interests, having the capacity "to fashion an appropriate remedy," is not inclined to do so.

To the extent government is not inclined to correct its deficiencies, we make a mockery out of the very definition of a tort—that is, any wrong for which government fashions an appropriate remedy.

The Health Industry

The health industry is a sixth of our economy. We cannot push it aside because the problems therein are complex and daunting and there are other problems more attractive to deal with, and far less difficult. A one-night stay in a hospital financially wipes out many an uninsured wage earner. The same night in a hospital can strip an elderly retired couple of a huge portion of their retirement savings. We have little trust in the government running a hospital, for example, the Veterans Administration. We tend to prefer private ownership and staffing. Survival under this system requires our agreement we will convert a significant portion of our earnings to insurance premiums, so we can spread the risk of staggering expenses.

Insurance has replaced health care in our discussions. Time and time again pundits wring their hands over the cost of insurance as opposed to the cost of health care. But we must acknowledge the fact the insurance company is not an altruistic nonprofit organization. The for-profit insurance company adds to this equation the need to make a profit for its shareholders. Reduced to its essentials, the insurance premium must cover all costs of operation, including such unsavory items as lobbying and litigation. Premium payers simply prepay for their later care and that of others in their class who take more than they contribute to the system.

A significant and burgeoning expense is tied up in litigation costs. Insurance companies acting in their own best interests have explored many avenues to keep premium payments down to a level where they are acceptable to the insured. The following suggestions are advanced:

First is compelling arbitration as an alternative to litigation. However, this remedy is between the insurance company and the premium payer. Absent a contract provision, it does not bind the injured plaintiff. For this contingency, it is possible to have an arbitration clause inserted into the patient/hospital contract.

Second is having the insured agree to assuming liability for the first $100,000 to $500,000 of any loss. Economics coerce the insured to bite off as much as they feel they can absorb. But as covered before, this gives rise to other problems. But neither of the above steps directly attacks the ever-burgeoning costs of medical care.

Third is that aside from the insurance factor, we might also consider the following to get a handle on these expenses of doing business:

- Put a cap on noneconomic or soft tissue (i.e., mental anguish). A reasonable cap should be placed on punitive damages. Whether a monetary cap or ratio to compensatory damages, there should be a limit. Between the two, they have become the tail that wags the dog.
- Modify the measure of liability to impose a fairer balance between the philosophies that no plaintiff go away empty-handed and that a defendant should only respond if culpable. As a first order of business, you must control junk expert testimony. You might consider having experts qualify before the court in advance of the trial, establishing exactly the field or fields in which they may express opinions. In a dispassionate hearing, the judge may exercise more control of the admissibility of opinion and conclusions, particularly if, when admitted, they go to the heart of the controversy.

During trial, these controversial discussions before a jury are likely to lead to unfortunate influence over the thought processes of the jury. Inadmissible matter from the expert or counsel by inadvertence or by design may well find its way into the jury room. Once blurted out in open court, it is all but impossible to unring the bell.

Two draconian measures in the eyes of those affected would be: award punitive damages to the state, not the plaintiff, and require that the loser pay all court costs and reasonable attorney fees to the prevailing party.

The benefits from these changes would be: Far fewer lawsuits would be filed. Far more disputes would be resolved by settlement. Doctors would not have to engage in defensive medicine to protect themselves from plaintiffs' lawyers. Medical care costs would dramatically be reduced. Doctors would not have to engage in needless procedures to intercept the malpractice lawyer looking over their shoulder. Legal services costs would understandably be reduced.

It is appropriate that we delve more deeply into doctors' frustrating problems.

"Just let me practice medicine" is the justifiable plea of physicians. They devote their lives to being doctors and now find themselves trying to master being secretaries filling out endless forms, chief financial officers trying to keep income within reach of ever-increasing costs of doing business, and wizards dealing with a government that constantly changes the rules of the game. Doctors are no longer masters of their own professional lives.

Doctors have no alternative. They are stuck with income from a single-payer system, without which they cannot survive. When one meets a patient for the first time, the doctor must ascertain what insurance program the patient has or what financial resources the patient has to ensure payment. This competes with what the doctor wants to do, which is find out what can medically be done for the patient.

Some unknown regulator has decided it is the doctor who must fill out certain forms. The doctor cannot have a secretary or assistant take this mindless administrative load away. This directly cuts into the time available to spend with patients.

"I am not, and don't want to be, a lawyer; just let me practice medicine," a doctor says. However, the doctor has no other alternative but to buy insurance as protection against the malpractice lawyer. The doctor must weigh the risk of a lawsuit against performing an unnecessary procedure. They call this "protective medicine." It drives up medical costs. Without this distasteful specter, the doctor would be free to exercise medical judgment without restraint.

"Please don't let an untrained bureaucrat second-guess my medical judgment; just let me practice medicine," the doctor says. Medical judgment is the foundation of and an integral part of the practice of medicine. While doctors welcome a second opinion from another qualified doctor, they deeply resent the insurers and bureaucrats, untrained in the practice of medicine and having considerations apart from the welfare of the patient, making decisions as to what is good for the patient. The bureaucrats and insurers have the hammer in that they will or will not pay for a procedure deemed inappropriate.

They are the ones who decide they will pay for only one procedure per day. Often more than one procedure is necessary. It poses no problem to the doctor to perform both procedures in one day. When patients travel considerable distances to get to their doctors, they must needlessly incur the expenses of staying overnight and returning to the office the next day for the second procedure. The restriction serves absolutely no purpose.

It is the bureaucrat and the insurer who, through regulations and rules, mandate the doctor personally fills out certain forms to be sent in and never to be looked at again. Compliance with their requirements is a prerequisite for the doctor to be paid.

We Have Lost Our Way

From the realistic, the practical, viewpoint in the real world, we have strayed from the reason for imposing liability. In the example set forth in appendix B, the goal or the objective of the judge, plaintiff's counsel, and defendant's counsel of record was to squeeze money out of the insured. This in spite of the unalterable facts that the insured was not responsible for the independent personal acts resulting in injury to the injured worker, nor were these acts within the scope of his employment

The system is not set up to resolve liability; it is set up to service the system by raising money. Counsel for the plaintiff was not about to contribute; the insurance company would not contribute, protected by the $400,000 cushion. The hospital that had a lien on an amount in excess of $75,000, extracted from the insured, had to be browbeaten into accepting ten cents on the dollar so there would be enough to pay off the worker's attorney; only then could the worker have the rest.

All this occurred because the judge and two counsel of record were not about to try the case and accept the result. The reason given was "that is just the way it is in these cases." That may well be the way it is, but it is not the way it should be.

Conclusion

If I were to reflect on what I have presented, I would be somewhat disappointed. It seems with every remedial avenue pursued, one ends up seeking relief from the very party who enjoys the benefits of the status quo they created.

As an example, we must look to attorneys to alleviate the time delays in litigation and the extraordinary costs. However, attorneys have a good point when they express their concern over trial calendars they have little or no control over and malpractice exposure if they don't make litigation expensive.

We look to doctors and hospitals to reduce the cost of their services to the ill and injured. But they justifiably argue, not only are we looking over our shoulders for the malpractice attorney but we are plagued with endless mindless regulations and insurance contracts we must comply with if we are to be paid. As we rapidly increase government interference, their position becomes increasingly hard to refute.

When we look to reduce the injustices that occur when citizens come into conflict with their government and are plunged into administrative law, we inevitably end up frustrated by entrenched interests in government that tip the scales in their favor, when citizens seek redress for injuries or relief from the impact of onerous regulations inflicted by government, its employees, or their agents.

The common thread is the shabby manner in which we appoint administrative law judges and how we allow them to function. However, there is a glimmer of hope for change here. The US Court of Appeals of the Tenth Circuit has rejected the manner in which administrative law judges function in the Securities Exchange Commission (SEC). Hopefully, the US Supreme Court will take the matter. This is a welcome start. Hopefully, it will eventually result in the elimination of the fraudulent practices described herein that deprive citizens of due process of law.

In the field of administrative law, we cannot reach the wrongdoers; we are relegated to complaining to our legislator. Our legislators are reduced to placating their constituents, arguing they alone are helpless to correct the problem. Underlying these problems that arise out of tortious conduct on the part of the regulator is disdain for Maguire and Zimet's admonition there is no reason why government "should not be held to a like standard of rectangular rectitude when dealing with its citizens."

This returns us to the distinction between our founders and the legislators today. Tort reform will not occur until we elect legislators with character. Character that insists on the same love of country exhibited by our founders.

On a much more cheerful concluding note, at some future time, the reader may well be enjoying the benefits of tort problems that have been legislatively reformed. The present federal administration has evidenced tort reform is one of the more important issues it will tackle and hopefully resolve. If it follows through, many of the frustrating problems set forth before will no longer plague us.

In the practice of law, I often concluded my arguments to the trial or appellate court with "I have said what I came to say. I'll gladly take questions." To the extent this book has provoked curiosity, thought, discussion, and questions, it has been a success.

Due Process Replaced

The first example deals with our NLRB (National Labor Relations Board). I represented a chain of nursing homes. The American Federation of Labor and Congress of Industrial Organizations (AFL-CIO) decided to organize in a nursing home having well in excess of one hundred beds. They forced a vote to have the union certified to represent them. They failed. They then decided to play hardball.

They gathered people from the streets of Sacramento, gave them prepared signs on sticks, and paid them a specified sum to picket the entrance to the facility, obstructing traffic, including tradespeople providing supplies to the facility and relatives of patients.

They then spread out on the driveway four pointed devices designed to puncture the tires of those who sought to pass. The object of this activity was to compel management to capitulate and submit to union representation.

Matters were brought to a head when a firebomb was thrown on the roof of a building housing a dozen patients who were not ambulatory. I was hired to bring these practices to a stop.

I filed a suit for injunctive relief, including a temporary restraining order and preliminary and permanent injunctive relief, and served the complaint on the union. In the meantime, the union quickly filed a complaint with the NLRB claiming unfair labor practices. The National Labor Relations Act provides one filing of a complaint with the board. The filer must first give ten days' written notice to the claimed offending party—in our case, the owner—to give that party a reasonable time to correct any conduct deemed offensive.

Counsel for the union simply backdated the notice to give him the required ten days' notice, but he mailed the notice well within the ten-day period. However, the post office placed its stamp, including the date, on the envelope, destroying the backdating deceptive stunt. I filed a motion with the NLRB to strike the complaint on the basis of a failure to give the required ten days' notice.

As a precaution, I made a copy of the stamped envelope, properly authenticated it, and filed it in support of the motion to strike.

At the hearing, the administrative law judge announced he would not accept a properly authenticated copy, that only the original envelope with the date stamp would be permitted. He then continued the matter. Now cautious, I prepared an affidavit for the signature of the Placer County Superior Court's county clerk, essentially stating that she was shown the original envelope and the filed envelope. They were identical. She attached another copy of the envelope to her affidavit. The original was then filed with the court.

At the second hearing, the judge asked if I had filed the original envelope. I said I had. He then asked the clerk to go through the file and find the original. Not surprisingly, it could not be found. They judge announced that as I hadn't produced the original, my motion must fail. At this point, I knew where everybody stood.

I then filed with the court the affidavit of the Placer County clerk. The look the judge gave counsel for the union was priceless. It told all: "Look what you got me into." The judge then put the NLRB matter over until further notice. In the meantime, the superior court trial proceeded to judgment against the union, who later agreed to a stipulated judgment prohibiting the union from engaging in any activity related to organizing the nursing home in question for five years.

Due Process Lost

I represented an airman who was a fixed-base operator and qualified to give check rides to others seeking to acquire FAA licenses. The administrator revoked his medical clearance for reasons not disclosed to the airman.

There were two separate trials to get his medical back. In the first, the airman lost his case before the administrative law judge. He appealed to the National Transportation Safety Board (NTSB). Shortly after filing the appeal, I received a phone call from the attorney representing the NTSB in the appellate proceedings. She got right to the point. The purpose of the call was to persuade me to drop the appeal. It was going nowhere. I naively advanced the proposition that the board, after considering the briefs and evidence, might look at matters differently and reverse the administrative law judge. This was the whole purpose of the appeal.

Her response was instructive although contemptuous. She lectured me, paraphrased as follows: "Do you really think the board is going to look at the evidence or briefs? They have much more important things to do. I will be writing the decision for them. If you drop the appeal, that will end it. If you don't, I will have to go to the trouble of preparing a brief in opposition to your opening brief, and I am not interested in going through that meaningless waste of time. You are not going win on appeal. I will be writing the decision, and all you are doing is putting me through the labor of having to prepare a brief in opposition to your appeal."

She was right on. I persisted in pursuing the appeal, lost, and then took the matter up through the US Court of Appeals for the Ninth Circuit, again losing.

About a year later, we made another trial effort, contesting the revocation of the airman's medical. After the matter was at issue and discovery could commence, I attempted to get the administrator's counsel to cooperate in disclosing the facts upon which the administrator had based his conclusion the airman posed a hazard to himself and others. I was first stalled and then rebuffed.

After being stiffed by the administrator's counsel, I sought relief through the administrative law judge who was handling the case, by filing a motion to produce this evidence, and received a signed order from the court requiring the administrator to provide his written evidence supporting his decision that the airman was a hazard to himself and others if permitted to fly.

The administrator ignored the order. After my repeated efforts, the administrator's counsel reluctantly agreed to allow the airman and his counsel to see the evidence. The airman and I were located in California so requested the administrator supply properly authenticated copies in lieu of having to incur the expense of traveling to the place where the FAA stored these documents.

The administrator's counsel refused. He demanded the airman and I come to Oklahoma City, to the FAA's office, to view the evidence. When I asked for a time for inspection, I was told the administrator had now moved the file to Washington, DC, and the airman and I would have to make the trip from San Francisco to Washington if we wanted to see the evidence.

Having no meaningful choice, I complied, and a time and place were established when we would show up in Washington, DC, at the NTSB office. The airman incurred this extraordinary unnecessary expense for the two of us to fly to Washington to view the documents. We showed up at the front desk of the NTSB at 10:00 a.m. to view the documents.

There followed a bizarre proceeding.

Nobody was manning the NTSB's front desk, so I waited. After ten minutes, I announced in a voice that could be heard by those chattering in the back room who we were and that we were here to view the documents the administrator was producing pursuant to the court order. When nothing happened, I advised the people in the back room we were not leaving and that somebody had best come out.

About twenty minutes after ten, a woman came out and announced the administrator had decided he would not produce the documents. When I served the court order on her, she laughingly announced, "We will have that rescinded before you get back to San Francisco." I advised her that any motion by the administrator to rescind or reverse would be opposed.

She contemptuously stated, "There will be no hearing. We will have the judge sign an order reversing your order. After all, his office is just two doors down the hall." Again, she was right on. The next day a signed new order from the judge reversing the original order was signed. No hearing, no notice, no argument, no nothing. So much for discovery, so much for due process.

Everything that transpired was reduced to the written record and made part of the court's file prior to trial, so when the inevitable appeal from an anticipated adverse decision occurred, the record on appeal would accurately and fully reflect how the administrator conducted business.

The trial went terribly wrong for the administrator. The administrative law judge held for the airman. One would reasonably suspect the reason the administrative law judge held for the airman was the administrator introduced a single letter in support of his position. This was the administrator's case. This anonymous letter appeared to have been written by a third party reflecting the airman's Sanford Hospital records.

The administrator apparently secured access to the airman's medical record. The letter's opening sentence purporting to set forth the physician's notes was: "Patient has a well-known history of cardiovascular disease." The date of the letter was sandwiched between the date of the airman's visit to the doctor and the date the intern later typed out the physician's notes for the file.

Stated differently, the physician's examination of the airman and his physician's notes were prepared on the tenth of the month. The administrator's letter was dated and represented by the administrator to have been sent on the fifteenth and received by the administrator within one or two days. The physician's secretary's typing of the notes took place on the twenty-fifth of the month.

The airman, upon seeing the letter, pointed out to me that the letter could not have been written on the fifteenth, that he had a copy of the physician's notes and they stated quite clearly: "Patient has no known history of cardiovascular disease."

After the administrator committed his authenticating witness to a date well before the nurse's notes were typed, the copy of the physician's notes was introduced into evidence, establishing the airman "had no known history of cardiovascular disease" as of the date the administrator testified he received the letter.

There was no way the administrator could wiggle off the hook. He had introduced into evidence a fraudulent document, a document that was the centerpiece of his case. This was the document the administrator refused to disclose prior to trial.

It is reasonable to conclude the administrative law judge did not want to see his name in print as a party to the administrator's fraud when the circuit court of appeals was handed the case and published its decision.

Aside from the administrator's introduction of fraudulent evidence, the hypocrisy of the administrator's behavior was compounded by an event that took place during this contentious proceeding. Another pilot who wanted to be certified with a check ride for an amphibious two-engine aircraft was pressing the administrator to produce a check ride instructor to administer the test. Only the check ride stood in the way of his acquiring the license. The only instructor in the region who was qualified to give this test was the very airman in question here.

The administrator saw no problem in authorizing the airman, whose medical ticket he had pulled, to give the check ride. At the time of the check ride, there was no qualified pilot in command of the aircraft. The airman whose medical had been pulled could not be pilot in command,

and the airman who was not qualified to pilot the aircraft could not be pilot in command. The administrator saw no hypocrisy in this duplicitous conduct.

Later, I had a long but cordial conversation with the doctor whose notes were in question. He apologized for the error. "She just misread my notes. In her defense, my handwriting is terrible." I assured him there was no problem; it had not affected the outcome.

APPENDIX C

Government Concealment and Deceit

To illustrate the problems that surface when government attempts to cover for the tortious conduct of its agent but, in aggressively pursuing its citizens, exacerbates the original wrong with further tortious conduct, I would like to present in detail an event that occurred about the time I was closing down my practice and retiring.

I represented a gyro repair facility (hereinafter the Gyro Shop). Pursuant to a contract with a private corporation, the Gyro Shop received six worn-out gyros with instructions to rebuild and certify them as airworthy. When it didn't prove economically feasible to rebuild these gyros and certify them (yellow tag them), with the concurrence of the buyer, the Gyro Shop acquired from Litton, the manufacturer of the original gyros, six other remanufactured gyros and resold these six remanufactured gyros to the Gyro Shop's buyer. Six remanufactured gyros left his facility to his buyer at a total cost of $36,000, or $6,000 per gyro.

These six worn-out gyros were taken from F-4 Phantom jet fighters. These gyros were specialty gyros and fit only in that aircraft. The Gyro Shop was later sued by a private individual in a qui tam suit on behalf the government (not a party to the transaction) for over $330,000, or over $50,000 per gyro, as that was what the government said they paid for these same six remanufactured gyros.

From the Gyro Shop's knowledge and perspective, there was nothing unusual about the transaction; the buyer sent the worn-out gyros to the Gyro Shop and wanted a price to rebuild and certify them. The Gyro Shop estimated it could rebuild the gyros economically but would have to pay $36,000 for the test equipment, which was necessary to test and yellow tag the gyros as airworthy. At $6,000 per gyro if the Gyro Shop rebuilt and tested the gyros, they would cost $10,000 to $12,000 per gyro.

When it appeared this was not feasible, the Gyro Shop owner suggested the buyer go directly to the original manufacturer, Litton Industries, and buy the remanufactured gyros directly from the manufacturer for $5,000 each. The buyer preferred the Gyro Shop handle the transaction with Litton, and it was agreed the Gyro Shop would charge $1,000 for each gyro for the service, for a total of $6,000 per gyro. To provide continuity in gyro identification when the remanufactured gyros were delivered to the ultimate buyer and installed in the F-4s, the buyer asked the Gyro Shop to put the nameplates from the old, worn-out gyros on the remanufactured gyros. The Gyro Shop complied.

As an aside, after winnowing out the chaff thrown up by the government's counsel that the gyros were in some manner defective, the only remaining complaint by the government was that the nameplates from the original worn-out gyros (the six that were too expensive to reman-ufacture) were placed on the remanufactured gyros. There was nothing misleading or illegal about this, as these gyros came with full documentation and certification that they were in fact remanufactured by Litton Industries and cer-tified as airworthy.

Whether a gyro works or not is not influenced, let alone controlled, by the numbers on the nameplate, whether it be the original numbers or new numbers or no numbers. The papers on each of these gyros goes into the file associated with the aircraft and allows anybody working on the gyro in the future to know where it came from and its history.

What is so disturbing about this transaction is that the government purchasing agent could have gone directly to Litton Industries—the manufacturer of the six worn-out gyros—and purchased remanufactured gyros for $5,000 each, or $30,000.

I was brought into the above controversy when the owner of the gyro facility advised me he needed help, as he had received notice from a government attorney that a complaint against him had been filed in Phoenix, Arizona, on behalf the government, claiming he had sold defective gyros to the government and American pilots were being subjected to injury or death.

The owner advised the government attorney to contact me, the owner's attorney. Shortly after, I received a phone call from the government attorney laying down the rules of the relationship between the gyro facility's owner and his government and, interestingly enough, what the owner's attorney could do and what he could not do. I was advised:

- A complaint against the gyro facility had been filed by a private party on behalf of the government. The claim concerned defective gyros sold to the government. These were defective, and as a result, Air Force pilots were placed in danger.
- The suit was what was referred to as a qui tam suit on behalf of the government, and the government was looking into whether to move in and take over the suit.
- When I asked the attorney to send me a copy of the complaint, his response was no; the file had been sealed, and nobody had access to it, including the owner of the gyro facility (the defendant) or his attorney.
- I could not discuss this suit with anybody, in particular the buyer of the gyros or its attorney.

- That government's counsel intended to ask my client, the owner, and his employees questions concerning the complaint. My cooperation and my client's were required or the government would triple the damages.

There followed a somewhat contentious dialogue between counsel. I advised him I had no problem with his interrogating my client; however, first, I wanted to see a copy of the complaint and go over it with my client. He advised me I could not see the complaint as the file was sealed. I told him he was the one who sealed the file and he was the one could open it. I said I would not produce anybody until I had received and digested the complaint.

He backed off and said he probably could send a copy of the complaint, but I could not discuss its contents with anybody, including my client, "because that's the law." I explained to him the first thing I intended to do when I received the complaint was to go over the complaint word-for-word with my client. He threatened to file a motion to hold me in contempt of court. I told him, "Be my guest; I'll be there."

I then explained that we did not want our defective gyros out there placing pilots in danger. So, I wanted to have a third party inspect the gyros to ferret out any defect, which we would promptly correct. He advised me that it would not be possible to produce the subject gyros for inspection.

What he concealed and did not disclose is equally important:

Notwithstanding the allegations in the complaint that alleged we delivered defective gyros, thereby subjecting American pilots to injury or death, he was aware the gyros would only fit in an F-4 Phantom no longer being manufactured or flown by American pilots, as the F-4 had been retired and replaced by F-16s over twenty years before. F-4s, upon being replaced, were mothballed or sent to our allies.

He had no evidence there was anything wrong with the gyros. Remember, he said he could not even produce the gyros for inspection. He simply had to have something to hang his hat on. His rejection of our request to inspect the gyros was premised upon his knowledge that these gyros were in F-4s Phantoms, mothballed, or being flown in Turkey or some other nation now flying the long-retired F-4s. When I pressed him to explain in detail exactly what was wrong with the gyros, he evaded.

He secreted the file for trial tactical purposes, completely unrelated to the only justification for allowing government to secret complaints on file with the federal district court from the public, including the defendant or his attorney. But it went further.

He had filed a similar complaint against others in the chain, from the gyro facility to his agent, seeking the same recovery from each. He demanded the gyro facility and its attorney not contact anybody up the chain, particularly the buyer of the gyros. This was premised upon his objective to keep all defendants apart, that is, in the dark, preventing them from discovering the shabby trial practice government was engaged in.

When the government attorney represented to me he couldn't produce the gyros he claimed were defective, he did not disclose they were probably already in the instrument panels of F-4s now owned by the Turkish air force or other allies, who were given or sold these aircraft when they were no longer of use to the United States. Disclosing this would have shattered his contention that American pilots were in danger. It also made it difficult for the Gyro Shop and other defendants to contact the owners of the F-4s and find out there was nothing wrong with the gyros.

This case was in the prepleading stage when I closed down my practice and turned the case over to competent counsel.

Glossary

administrative law courts: Trial courts created within legislative acts to dispose of disputes arising out of the legislation.

adversarial system: A system adopted by the United States wherein each party advances its cause either directly or through attorneys, to a trier of fact; the judge's role is reduced to that of a nonpartisan referee. Distinguish from the *inquisitorial system*.

arbitration: An alternative to an Article III trial court or administrative law court, where the parties agree the matter can be decided by a mutually acceptable third party.

Article III courts: Article III of our Constitution provides for a federal court system consisting of the trial courts, appellate courts, and the Supreme Court. It also provides states may do the same. Each state has created a trial court, appellate courts, and one supreme court. Therefore, we have two Article III court systems operating side by side.

beneficiary: Person(s) for whom a trust relationship is created, with benefits.

burden of proof: The law imposes a burden to introduce evidence proving a fact material to the party's case. The burden may vary. In a criminal matter, we require the prosecution to prove each element beyond a reasonable doubt. In a civil action, the measure is the preponderance of evidence. In a tort action, the plaintiff must prove each element in the cause of action by the preponderance of evidence.

CCP: California's Civil Code of Procedure.

Circuit Court of Appeals (CCA): Courts that review district court decisions to ascertain whether there is error that appears in the record.

collateral source rule: The collateral source rule prevents a defendant from introducing evidence that the plaintiff already has been compensated partially or in full for the injury caused by the defendant.

common law: English judge-made law, as opposed to legislative law, carried over and made a part of our law.

complaint: The initial pleading in a lawsuit in which plaintiffs set forth the facts upon which they claim relief. The responsive pleading may be an answer admitting or denying allegations in the complaint or alleging that even if we assume the facts are true, the complaint does not set forth sufficient facts to warrant relief or some affirmative defense applies.

condemnation or eminent domain: The right of government to take private property for a public purpose or use, after paying just compensation.

continuance: A court-granted extension of time from the date initially set for a proceeding.

deposition: The oral examination of a party or witness.

demurrer: Even if what you allege is true, your complaint does not set forth sufficient facts to state a cause of action.

discovery: Legislative tools provided to parties, allowing them to ascertain from their adversary facts and theories of the case.

due process: A term found in our Fifth and Fourteenth Amendments, succinctly defined as reasonable notice and an opportunity to be heard.

easement: An interest in real property permitting a specified use on another's property.

equity: When a court sits in equity, it applies equitable principles, as opposed to applying a legislative act.

federal district court: The trial courts in the federal system.

fee simple: All interests or rights in real property.

fiduciary: One who stands in trust to a beneficiary, obliged to act in the best interests of the beneficiary (e.g., an attorney to the client, a doctor to the patient, a trustee to the beneficiary).

HIPPA: Health Insurance Portability and Accountability Act.

indemnity: One who is secondarily liable has a right to require the primary tortfeasor to hold the secondary harmless from any loss suffered as result of the primary's wrongful conduct.

inquisitorial system: Distinguished from the adversarial system, in that the judge takes a more active role in a trial proceeding. The judge, not the attorneys, examines the witnesses.

interrogatories: Questions lodged by one party to another inquiring into facts relevant to the case.

joint liability: Each defendant, if jointly liable, is responsible for the whole of any judgment arising out of tort litigation.

legislative body: The entity having the power to make laws that govern people.

lien: The legally enforceable right to do something to or on another's property, such as a recorded judgment lien, a deeded lien to cross another person's property.

malpractice: The failure of a person to exercise reasonable care in performing their obligations or duty owed to another.

Need and Necessity Resolution: The enactment by a governmental body authorizes the condemnation of property by legislatively finding there is need for the property, and it is necessary to complete a public project.

negligence: Failure to adhere to an established standard of care.

nonjusticiable: A legislative or executive matter not judicial; therefore, the court will not look into or decide the matter.

plaintiffs' bar: An association of attorneys specializing in tort litigation.

promisor: One who makes an enforceable promise.

promisor, express: A promisor who overtly makes the representation.

promisor, implied: A promisor who indirectly suggests the representation.

proximate cause: The legally recognized cause of the plaintiff's injury.

punitive damages: Damages awarded to the plaintiff in addition to compensatory damages to punish the wrongdoer and inhibit further like conduct on the part of others.

quasi-court: A term applied to judicially binding proceedings outside the Article III court system.

quasi-judicial: A determination by a quasi-court (e.g., an administrative law court).

qui tam suit: A legislatively-provided-for court proceeding where a citizen can file a complaint on behalf of the government, ostensibly enforcing a government cause of action. The government can then choose to take over the litigation, or the private citizen complainant can proceed.

quid pro quo: Bargained for exchange.

rectangular rectitude: Turn square corners, or play it straight when dealing with others.

res ipsa loquitur: A shifting of the plaintiff's burden of proof to the defendant(s) under circumstances where the plaintiff cannot be expected to be aware of facts known only by the defendant(s).

right of contribution: Defendants who pay more than their allocated share of the total judgment attributable to their wrongful conduct and are entitled to contribution from other defendants, to the end that all defendants pay only that percentage of the total judgment attributable to their wrongful conduct.

self-governance: When people govern themselves, usually in a republic through elected representatives.

self-insure: In lieu of having the insurance company cover the whole of the loss, the insured may agree to assume a first portion of that exposure, up to an agreed-upon limit.

several liability: Where each defendant is responsible for only that percentage of the total wrongful conduct attributable to that defendant.

single-payer system: A term describing what we have morphed into when we no longer pay the physician or hospital directly for medical services.

sovereign: No higher authority.

special assessment district: A public entity formed by government to perform a specific project and financed by those properties who will be specially benefited from the project.

statutory law: Law from a legislature or legislative body.

statute of limitations: A time limitation placed on a party to perform an act, such as filing a complaint or bringing the matter to trial.

stare decisis: Adherence to prior law or established principle.

substantial evidence: Admissible, relevant material evidence.

summary judgment: An independent proceeding where a party may move the court for judgment upon the premise there is no factual dispute on one or all of the controlling or dispositive issues.

tort: Any wrongful conduct for which the law fashions an appropriate remedy.

tortfeasor: One who engages in wrongful conduct.

trier of facts: In a trial, one who determines the existence of or at times the nonexistence of the ultimate facts. It may be a jury or judge or an agreed-upon arbitrator. If a jury is the trier of facts, the judge then applies the law. If the trier of facts is either the judge or arbitrator, they perform both functions.

venue: The location(s) where the court has jurisdiction over the thing, event, or parties.

warranty: When one guarantees a product will perform as represented.

warranty, express: An overt express representation of fact.

warranty, implied: A representation of fact made indirectly as a suggestion, or inference.

Index

In this index, definitions of terms are in **bold page numbers**.

United States Supreme Court (USSC), 15, 51–52, 76, 87–90, 95

V
venue, 9, 150, **157**

W
Wade, John D., 17–18
waiver of immunity, 86–90
warranties: definition of term, **157–158**; express warranties, 21, 27–28, **158**; implied warranties, 21–22, 28; manufacture of goods and, 2, 18, 21–24, 27–28; recovery upon warranty, 16–17, 24–28, 50, 108–109; responsibility *vs.* compensation and, 43–44; strict liability and, 24–28
Washington, George, 102, 103
workers' compensation case, 63–68, 69
wrongful conduct, 7, 24, 28, 44–45, 47, 49–53, 85–90, **156, 157**

Z
Zimet, Phillip, 119–120, 130

About the Author

A graduate of University of California Hastings College of the Law, James K. Norman was a practicing trial lawyer for thirty-five years. During this time, he handled cases relating to constitutional law; business law; environmental problems; residential, commercial, and industrial construction problems; local government; and administrative law.

At the University of Iowa, he lettered in track, tennis, and gymnastics, acquiring Big Ten and national titles. In 1997, after retiring, he began devoting his time to teaching the United States Constitution to high school students and to the elderly. He is also a retired United States Coast Guard Reserve lieutenant commander.

Born and raised in Iowa, Norman currently resides in Idaho with his wife, La Donna.

CPSIA information can be obtained
at www.ICGtesting.com
Printed in the USA
FSHW02n0151270618
49568FS